LEADING WOMEN

Ruth Bader Ginsburg

Supreme
Court
Justice

CATHLEEN SMALL

Cavendish
Square
New York

Published in 2018 by Cavendish Square Publishing, LLC
243 5th Avenue, Suite 136, New York, NY 10016

Website: cavendishsq.com

Library of Congress Cataloging-in-Publication Data

Names: Small, Cathleen, author.
Title: Ruth Bader Ginsburg : Supreme Court Justice / Cathleen Small.
Description: New York : Cavendish Square Publishing, [2018] |
Series: Leading women | Includes bibliographical references and index.
Identifiers: LCCN 2016053712 (print) | LCCN 2016055193 (ebook) |
ISBN 9781502626974 (library bound) | ISBN 9781502626981 (E-book)
Subjects: LCSH: Ginsburg, Ruth Bader. |
Women judges--United States--Biography. | Judges--United States--Biography. |
United States. Supreme Court--Officials and employees--Biography.
Classification: LCC KF8745.G56 S63 2018 (print) | LCC KF8745.G56 (ebook) |
DDC 347.73/2634 [B] --dc23
LC record available at https://lccn.loc.gov/2016053712

Editorial Director: David McNamara
Editor: Tracey Maciejewski
Copy Editor: Nathan Heidelberger
Associate Art Director: Amy Greenan
Designer: Lindsey Auten
Production Coordinator: Karol Szymczuk
Photo Research: J8 Media

Printed in the United States of America

CONTENTS

CHAPTER ONE

Ruth Bader: Destined for Leadership

Ruth Bader Ginsburg is currently the oldest member of the United States Supreme Court, but more than that, she is known for her liberal views and her sharp tongue when it comes to pointing out injustices that she sees. Examining her early life in Brooklyn and later at Harvard and Columbia Law Schools provides some insight into the forces that shaped this young Jewish girl into the Notorious R.B.G.

Ruth Bader Ginsburg at the taping of *The Kalb Report*, a monthly Nation Press Club forum on media ethics and responsibility

Early Family Life in Brooklyn

The woman who would become Ruth Bader Ginsburg, the second female justice appointed to the United States Supreme Court (and the first female Jew to be appointed to the prestigious position), began life in the Flatbush neighborhood of Brooklyn, New York, on March 15, 1933, where she was born Ruth Joan Bader. Although Flatbush is now made up primarily of African American and West Indian families, in the early 1900s, it was a working-class part of Brooklyn filled with Irish American, Italian American, and Jewish families. Ruth's Jewish immigrant parents fit in well in the diverse neighborhood, where they were members of the East Midwood Jewish Center.

Ruth's father, Nathan Bader, emigrated from Russia when he was thirteen years old. As an adult, he was a **furrier** and later a **haberdasher**, and though he was reasonably successful in his careers, he did not have a high school education.

On the other hand, his wife, Celia Bader (formerly Amster), had a strong interest in education. She was born in the United States to parents who had emigrated from a town near Krakow, Poland, shortly before their daughter's birth. Celia had a high school education (and her strong intellect had allowed her to graduate at age fifteen), but she was not able to go to college—not many women went to college in Celia's time, and her family chose to send Celia's brother instead of her. Celia worked in a garment factory to earn money to put toward her brother's education.

As a wife to Nathan and a mother to their children, Celia did not pursue a career of her own, but she was a homemaker and helped out in Nathan's businesses. She never lost her love of learning, which she instilled in her daughter, Ruth. Celia took Ruth to the library every week to ensure that she had plenty of reading material. The library happened to be housed above a Chinese restaurant, and even now Ruth says that the smell of Chinese food reminds her how much she enjoys reading. "One of my greatest pleasures as a child was sitting on my mother's lap when she would read to me, and then going to the library with her," Ruth remembers.[1]

It was through these early library trips that Ruth learned about courageous, independent women. In an era when little girls were expected to grow up to become wives and raise families of their own, Ruth delighted in books about pioneering aviator Amelia Earhart, the Greek goddess Athena, and fictional female detective Nancy Drew. Her reading and her mother's encouragement to be an independent thinker were major influences on Ruth, who grew up poised to challenge a system that reinforced gender stereotypes. "My mother told me to be a lady. And for her, that meant be your own person, be independent," Ruth has remarked.

In addition to a love of reading and education, Celia also imbued in Ruth a spirit of independence, idealism, and thriftiness. Ruth vividly recalls bargain shopping with her mother so that the family could save money for Ruth's future college education.

Although Celia died before Ruth reached adulthood, she remains one of Ruth's biggest influences. Of her late mother, Ruth has said, "I think of her often when I am in challenging situations that compel a top performance."[2]

Early Tragedy

Although Ruth had a strong childhood with positive role models in both of her parents, her childhood was not without tragedy. Ruth wasn't Celia and Nathan's only child; rather, she was their second daughter. The Baders' eldest daughter, Marilyn, died of meningitis at age six, when Ruth was just two years old. Although Ruth was too young when her sister died to really remember her, Marilyn was the one who bestowed the nickname "Kiki" on Ruth—a nickname that stuck throughout Ruth's childhood and into her time at Camp Che-Na-Wah in the Adirondacks, where she acted as the camp rabbi when she was a young teenager.

The specter of World War II and Hitler's persecution of Jews loomed over Ruth's childhood, given that she was born in 1933, at the beginning of Hitler's rise to power. The news of Jews being persecuted by Nazis was a topic of conversation in her family, and Ruth was aware of discrimination against Jews in the United States even at a young age. During her confirmation hearings for the Supreme Court, Senator Edward Kennedy voiced concern that her background in gender discrimination might make her particularly sensitive to racial discrimination as well. Ruth replied:

I am alert to discrimination. I grew up during World War II in a Jewish family. I have memories as a child, even before the war, of being in a car with my parents and passing a place in [Pennsylvania], a resort with a sign out front that read: "No dogs or Jews allowed." Signs of that kind existed in this country during my childhood. One couldn't help but be sensitive to discrimination living as a Jew in America at the time of World War II.[3]

Amid the specter of war, the family was faced with tragedy again, when Ruth was a freshman in high school and Celia was diagnosed with cervical cancer. Celia fought the disease throughout Ruth's time as a student at James Madison High School, but she succumbed to it the day before Ruth's graduation, where Ruth had been scheduled to speak. Due to her mother's passing, Ruth missed her high school graduation, and her diploma and medals had to be delivered to her at a later time.

It was a difficult blow for the family, particularly given the timing. Celia had been such a champion for Ruth's education and had dreamed of seeing her daughter go to college and become a history teacher. Unfortunately, that dream didn't become a reality for Celia.

But Celia has always remained an inspiration to Ruth. When Ruth was nominated to the Supreme Court, she spoke of Celia, saying she was "the bravest and strongest person I have known … I pray that I may be all that she would have been had she lived in an age when women could aspire and achieve and daughters are cherished as much as sons."[4] She has quietly paid homage to her mother's memory for more than six decades by wearing Celia's jewelry whenever she appears at the Supreme Court. In some ways, those early tragedies may have helped prepare Ruth for some of the challenges she would face later on in her life.

School and the Teenage Years

As an adult, Ruth is known for being quite serious. However, she wasn't always that way—in fact, she was quite a popular student. Before she went on to study at Cornell University, she was a member of the honor society in high school—but also a member of the pep squad! She was also a baton twirler and played cello in her school orchestra.

As a child, Ruth attended Public School 238 in Brooklyn and later James Madison High School, also in Brooklyn. Ruth was known as a bright student who always did well on tests, despite being modest and **self-effacing**.

CLASS
OF
JUNE 1946
P. S. 238
BROOKLYN

A young Ruth Bader with her class in 1946

In PS 238, she was the editor of the *Highway Herald*, and her editorials on the Magna Carta and the Bill of Rights were an early indicator of the analytical mind that would lead her to excel in the field of law.

Her propensity to challenge the system was fully evident in those early years, too. Ruth, who is left-handed, reportedly was vocal in her disagreement with a school rule that said children must write with their right hands!

The College and Law School Years

After a promising school career throughout primary school and high school, Ruth moved on to Cornell University in Ithaca, New York. Her mother had managed to save $8,000 (which would equate to roughly $80,000 in today's dollars) toward Ruth's education, but Ruth won enough scholarships that she was able to give that money to her father instead.

At Cornell, Ruth was a member of Jewish sorority Alpha Epsilon Phi. She graduated from the university with a degree in government (with high honors) in 1954; she also graduated with distinction in all other subjects she studied.

During her time at Cornell, Ruth's interest in law was piqued. It was the era of **McCarthyism**, and Ruth was disturbed by Senator Joseph McCarthy's attempts to curb free speech and thought among American citizens. Lawyers, Ruth realized, could fight back against this type of censorship, as well as against the religious discrimination she had seen while growing up Jewish during the war years and the gender discrimination she saw every day as a woman pursuing higher education and eventually a career in a male-dominated era.

Perhaps the icing on the cake of her time at Cornell, though, was meeting her future husband, Martin Ginsburg, a fellow Cornell student who was a year ahead of her in school. The two met on a blind date, and they married in July 1954, shortly after Ruth graduated. Ruth didn't attend Cornell in search of a husband, but years later she wryly noted, "I went to Cornell. It was the school for parents who wanted to make sure their girl would find a man. Four guys for every woman. If you came out without a husband, you were hopeless."[5]

Early in their marriage, Ruth moved to Fort Sill, Oklahoma, where her new husband was completing his military service as an ROTC officer in the Army Reserve who had been called to duty. Ruth worked for the Social Security office in Oklahoma at that time, but she found herself demoted after becoming pregnant with the couple's first daughter, Jane. It was just one of many instances of gender discrimination Ruth would witness over the years.

Yet another instance occurred after Martin was discharged from service, when the young couple moved to the Boston area so Martin could begin law school at Harvard. Ruth followed her husband into law school at Harvard, where she was one of only nine women in a class of five hundred. The dean of Harvard Law School invited all nine women in the class to a dinner and asked them, "How do you justify taking a spot [in the prestigious law school] from a qualified man?" Ruth said she gave the dean "the answer he expected," saying, "My husband is a second-year law student, and it's important for a woman to understand her husband's work." In a 2015 *New York Times* interview, Ruth was asked if she actually believed the reason she gave for attending Harvard Law. "Of course not!" she replied, and went on to express her discontent with another practice at the time: "They had given me a generous scholarship. We had to take two years off when Marty was in the service. And when I applied for readmission, they said, 'Submit your father-in-law's financial statement.' They shouldn't give scholarship funds to a person with family money, but you can be sure they never asked a guy to submit his father-in-law's statement!"[6]

During their time at Harvard, Martin was diagnosed with testicular cancer and had to undergo treatment. Thankfully, the treatment was successful, but it added yet another dimension to Ruth's already full plate. While Martin was ill, Ruth attended her own classes plus all of Martin's, and she typed up all his papers, all while tending to her ill husband and raising their young daughter. Somehow, she still managed to win a spot in the *Harvard Law Review*.

Once recovered from his illness, Martin received a job offer in New York City, and Ruth transferred to Columbia Law School to finish her studies. While at Columbia, Ruth also won a seat on their law review. She was the first law student to have sat on both the *Harvard Law Review* and the *Columbia Law Review*. Ultimately, Ruth graduated first in her class at Columbia, tied with one other student.

Martin Ginsburg, circa 1993

After Graduation

With such an impressive record, Ruth should have been a shoo-in for any job she wanted. But such was not the case in 1959, when feminism had not yet taken hold and broken many barriers for women seeking careers outside of teaching. Ruth interviewed at twelve law firms after graduating from Columbia, and not a single one offered her employment. Harvard professor Albert Sachs personally recommended Ruth to Supreme Court Justice Felix Frankfurter, but despite the glowing review, Frankfurter refused to offer her the position of law clerk.

Ruth remembers that time, saying, "There were many [law] firms who put up sign-up sheets that said, 'Men Only.' And I had three strikes against me. First, I was Jewish, and the Wall Street firms were just beginning to accept Jews. Then I was a woman. But the killer was my daughter Jane, who was four by then."[7]

Ruth eventually gained experience by clerking for two years for Judge Edmund G. Palmieri of the US District Court for the Southern District of New York, and that led her to receive offers of employment from several law firms. But instead, Ruth decided to accept a position as associate director for Columbia Law School's Project on International Procedure. This led her to learn Swedish and travel to Sweden to study their legal system (which was more female-friendly than the legal profession in the United States at that time). Shortly thereafter, Ruth began to teach law at Rutgers University in New Jersey, where she was one of fewer than twenty female law professors in the entire United States—and where she once again faced gender

A Notorious Nickname

Justice Ruth Bader Ginsburg has earned herself a cult following because of her outspoken, liberal views and her pioneering work on women's and **LGBTQ** rights. Her no-nonsense approach to evaluating and analyzing law has led some to refer to her as "the Notorious R.B.G."–a play on the late rapper Notorious B.I.G. It's easy to see how her early influences and experiences shaped the young, intelligent Ruth Bader into the fierce Notorious R.B.G. who currently sits as the oldest member on the United States Supreme Court.

discrimination when she was told that she would receive a lower salary than a male professor because her husband had a well-paying job.

It was there that Ruth gave birth to her and Martin's second child, a son named James. Ruth reportedly wore loose clothing to hide her pregnancy for as long as possible, having faced discrimination when she revealed her pregnancy with Jane a decade earlier.

CHAPTER TWO

Early Successes

Despite a stunning career at Cornell University, Harvard Law School, and Columbia Law School, Ruth Bader Ginsburg faced difficulty entering her professional career—because she was a woman, because she was Jewish, and because she was a mother. Nevertheless, her early years in the legal profession are peppered with successes that ultimately led to her iconic career as a Supreme Court justice.

Collegiate Success at Cornell

Ginsburg joked about Cornell being the university you went to if your parents wanted to ensure that you found

Cornell University in Ithaca, New York, where Ginsburg received her undergraduate degree a husband, but she had a very successful four years at the university. In addition to graduating with a Bachelor of Arts degree with high honors in government and with distinction in all subjects, Ginsburg graduated Phi Beta Kappa and Phi Kappa Phi.

Phi Beta Kappa is an elite honor society in the arts and sciences that was founded in 1776. It has chapters at only about 10 percent of United States universities. At those institutions, only about 10 percent of graduates in the arts and sciences are invited to join. Needless to say, being invited to join this honor society is quite a feather in one's cap, and Ginsburg is in distinguished company as a Phi Beta Kappa graduate; members include 17 US presidents, 39 Supreme Court justices (Ginsburg being one), and more than 130 Nobel Laureates.

Phi Kappa Phi is also an honor society, like Phi Beta Kappa. It was founded in 1897 and claims to be the most selective multidisciplinary collegiate honor society, with its emphasis on recognizing superior scholarship across disciplines. Notable members of Phi Kappa Phi include Pulitzer Prize winners, Nobel Prize winners, presidents, and other politicians.

A Law-School Star

Ruth Bader Ginsburg attended two law schools. Ginsburg says she chose to attend law school "for personal, selfish reasons. I thought I could do a lawyer's job better than any other. I have no talent in the arts, but I do write fairly well and analyze problems clearly."[1]

She began her studies at Harvard Law but completed them at Columbia Law School, after her husband, Martin, accepted a job in New York City. At both law schools—which, it should be noted, are two of the most prestigious law schools in the nation—Ginsburg was at the top of her class and won spots on the law reviews.

The *Harvard Law Review* is a monthly publication run by students at Harvard Law School. It is intended to be a practical research tool for lawyers and legal students, but it's also a way for members of the *Review* to practice and refine their writing skills—crucial for a future lawyer. Harvard Law students, like Ruth Bader Ginsburg, are the editors of the *Review*, and it's not as simple as just wanting to work on a school newspaper. Members are selected based on an annual writing competition, and the contest for a seat on the *Review* is fierce. Winning a spot is a notable accomplishment to put on one's resume—only forty-six editors are invited to join each year. Remember that Ginsburg was one in a class of five hundred students, and you can do the math. You have to be one of the elite students to win a coveted spot. Ginsburg is in prestigious company as a former editor of the *Review*. Her fellow Supreme Court justice Elena Kagan was a supervising editor on the *Review*, as was President Barack Obama.

While receiving an honorary degree from Harvard University in 2011, the opera-loving Ginsburg was serenaded by Placido Domingo.

The *Columbia Law Review* is similar to the *Harvard Law Review* in structure—it's a student-run law journal that is widely published and cited by legal professionals. As with the *Harvard Law Review*, gaining a seat on the *Columbia Law Review* is a feather in one's professional cap. Ginsburg's fellow Supreme Court justice William O. Douglas is a former member, as are countless other legal professionals, well-known law professors, and politicians.

The fact that Ginsburg served on *both* noteworthy publications is nothing short of amazing—she was the first person to do so.

Ginsburg tied for the top of her graduating class at Columbia Law School, and she also was named a Kent scholar—another prestigious accolade. Kent scholars are recognized for their outstanding academic achievement at Columbia Law School. Kent scholars are typically in the top 8 percent of their class at Columbia Law—which was no problem for Ginsburg, who was tied for top honors in her class. In 2011, Columbia Law School instituted the Ruth Bader Ginsburg Prize, which is awarded annually to degree candidates who are Kent scholars for all three years.

The student she tied with, by the way, was a young man named Richard Givens. Remembering his fellow Columbia Law rival, he says Ginsburg was "very brilliant, incisive, quick and thoughtful."[2]

Study of Sweden

Despite her many successes at Cornell, Harvard, and Columbia, Ginsburg struggled to enter the professional world. She was turned down by numerous law firms that weren't shy about refusing her on the basis of her being Jewish, female, a mother, or a combination of the three. Eventually, she took a clerk position for Judge Edmund L. Palmieri, and she held that position for two years.

At that point, Ginsburg returned to Columbia to join the Project on International Procedure, along with

Professor Hans Smit. The overall goal of the people involved in the project was to research foreign civil procedure and then propose transnational litigation rules for the United States. As her part of that project, Ginsburg learned Swedish so that she could coauthor a book on Sweden's legal system, along with a Swedish judge.

Ginsburg says that this project, which she worked on in 1962 and 1963, is what caused her to begin thinking seriously about women's equality. Having been one of nine women in a law school class of five hundred, Ginsburg was surprised to see that between 20 and 25 percent of law students in Sweden were female. And more astonishingly, there were female judges presiding on the bench in Sweden—while the highly acclaimed Ginsburg couldn't even secure a clerkship with most law firms in the United States. Ginsburg remembers seeing a presiding judge in Stockholm who was eight months pregnant while on the bench—while in the United States, Ginsburg had been demoted in a government job for being pregnant just a few years before.

But Ginsburg noted that it wasn't a perfect situation in Sweden, either. Women worked in the law profession, but it wasn't so much a matter of the Swedes being particularly progressive with regard to women's rights—it was more a matter of necessity. Says Ginsburg of the situation, "Inflation was high [in Sweden], and two incomes were often needed. But it was the woman who was expected to buy the kids new shoes and have dinner on the table at 7."[3] Ginsburg also remembers reading the writing of a Swedish journalist who commented that women often had two jobs, whereas men only had one.

So the gender situation was different in Sweden— but the grass wasn't necessarily greener. Women could work in more diverse careers, but it certainly wasn't an equitable situation.

The legal textbook that had led Ginsburg to Sweden was entitled *Civil Procedure in Sweden*, and it was published in 1965. Just five years later, in 1970, Ginsburg entered the publishing forum again when she cofounded the *Women's Rights Law Reporter*, the first and longest-running legal periodical in the United States that focuses exclusively on women's rights law.

Beginnings as a Feminist Icon

Although Ginsburg's time as a student at Columbia Law School had been exemplary and she was well regarded for her work on the Project on International Procedure, Ginsburg was not offered a faculty position at Columbia. Instead, she went to Rutgers Law School in Newark, New Jersey, where she was a professor of law for nine years. It wasn't until 1972, thirteen years after her graduation at the top of her Columbia Law School class, that Ginsburg was offered a position at her alma mater. When she accepted that position, she became Columbia Law School's first tenured female professor.

A Progressive Partner

Ginsburg's biggest ally in the fight for equal rights for women may have been her own husband, Martin. Although Martin was a brilliant attorney in his own right, he often played second fiddle to his much better known wife. That began early in their lives, when Martin did not make the *Harvard Law Review* but Ginsburg did—a fact that he was immensely proud of, along with almost all of his wife's accomplishments. In a note he wrote to Ruth just ten days before he died from metastatic cancer in 2010, Martin wrote, "I have admired and loved you almost since the day we first met at Cornell some 56 years ago. What a treat it has been to watch you progress to the very top of the legal world!"[4]

In their home life, Ruth and Martin were known as true partners with common goals. While Ruth left Harvard Law for Columbia when Martin got a job in New York, the situation was reversed later, when Martin moved to Washington, DC, to support a career move for Ruth. And while raising their family, they kept an even balance on which parent would do the childcare while the other focused on work at any given time.

The two had an agreement that both would be home every night for dinner with their children, except in extreme circumstances. They held true to that agreement as their children grew up.

As for household duties, the two split them fairly evenly, though Martin was known to be the far better cook, and thus he took the lead on that. He became well known for the dinners he would prepare for

Justice Ginsburg and her husband, children, and grandchildren, circa 1993

Ginsburg's law clerks once each term, and he was known for baking a cake on each law clerk's birthday, too. In her typical no-nonsense way, Ginsburg would leave a note for the clerk: "It's your birthday, so Marty baked a cake."[5] Today, the Supreme Court gift shop offers some insight into Martin's love of cooking with *Chef Supreme: Martin Ginsburg*, a cookbook put together by the spouses of the other Supreme Court justices as a tribute to Martin Ginsburg after his death in 2010.

In a **patriarchal** era, Martin and Ruth were unique in their division of labor and parenting. They lived the very kind of equality that Ruth later became famous for promoting.

Ginsburg at the 1999 dedication for the Center for Law and Justice at Rutgers University

Ginsburg's time at Rutgers was noteworthy. She wasn't simply passing time between stints at Columbia. Her interest in gender equality and women's rights had been sparked during her time in Sweden, though it had been germinating since her childhood, when she gravitated toward books with strong female subjects. While at Rutgers, Ginsburg was one of only two female law professors there. In fact, there were only a few female law professors in the entire country!

When a group of students from Rutgers Law School asked her to lead a seminar on women and the law in the late 1960s, it was a natural yes for Ginsburg. She quickly set about preparing for the class and realized that there wasn't much legal precedent to study. In fact, she found a sizable gap at the intersection between law and gender equality. Ginsburg says of that seminar, "Rutgers students sparked my interest and aided in charting the course I then pursued. Less than three years after starting the seminar, I was arguing gender discrimination cases before the Supreme Court."[6]

While often teachers inspire students, in this case it was the students who inspired their teacher—and led her to become a pioneer in women's rights and gender equality.

Ginsburg's interest in the subject didn't escape the attention of the New Jersey chapter of the American Civil Liberties Union (**ACLU**). By this point, the Civil Rights Act had become law, and women were beginning to report gender discrimination that they felt violated their civil rights. For example, a woman was asked to leave her job when her pregnancy became noticeable. A factory worker was told her company's health insurance was only available to male employees. A Princeton engineering program for children was only open to boys.

Knowing Ginsburg's interest in gender equality and women's rights, the ACLU asked Ginsburg to handle the cases they were getting. Ginsburg was intrigued, feeling that men and women could "create new traditions by their actions, if artificial barriers [were] removed, and avenues of opportunity held open to them."[7] Ginsburg wanted to be involved in removing those barriers and holding open the avenues of opportunity.

In 1971, as part of her work for the ACLU, Ginsburg authored the legal **brief** for *Reed v. Reed*—her first Supreme Court brief—which turned out to be a landmark decision for women's rights. The case involved a statute on estate administration that was deemed unconstitutional because it discriminated based on gender, and Ginsburg's brief was instrumental in the Supreme Court's ultimate decision—a pivotal moment in the history of women's rights and law. Not long after, the ACLU named Ginsburg the co-director of their newly created Women's Rights Project, which was dedicated to gender discrimination litigation.

At this time, critics of the women's liberation movement took issue with complaints such as these and said that women's liberation activists were simply trying to ride on the coattails of civil rights activists. However, notable feminists such as Gloria Steinem disagreed. Steinem insisted that the women's liberation and civil rights movements were "profoundly connected. If you are going to continue racism, you have to control reproduction. And that means controlling women."[8]

Ginsburg, too, saw the movements as connected. She alluded to this in 1971, when she added to her brief for *Reed v. Reed* the name of black civil rights activist and lawyer Pauli Murray. Ginsburg reportedly wanted to be clear that she was "standing on [the] shoulders" of those who had fought before her.[9] And during her testimony at the 1993 nomination hearings for her seat on the Supreme Court, Ginsburg again linked feminism with civil rights and paid homage to influential women in both debates:

> *I surely would not be in this room today without the determined efforts of men and woman who kept dreams of equal citizenship alive in days when few would listen. People like Susan B. Anthony, Elizabeth Cady Stanton and Harriet Tubman come to mind. I stand on the shoulders of those brave people.[10]*

Steinem and Ginsburg became acquainted by way of an ACLU case that Ginsburg was working on, in which African American women were being sterilized without their permission. Says Ginsburg of the case, "There was this notorious obstetrician, and if it was a [black] woman's third child, he would automatically sterilize her."[11] Steinem knew Ginsburg as a champion for women's rights through her work with the ACLU, and Ginsburg knew Steinem because she was a devoted reader of *Ms.* magazine, a liberal feminist magazine that Steinem cofounded in the early 1970s.

Ruth Bader Ginsburg was only just beginning her entry into the public eye. But it wouldn't be long before her name was known in much wider circles.

CHAPTER THREE

The Public Eye

While Ginsburg was well known in legal circuits around Harvard, Columbia, and Rutgers in the 1960s, in the early 1970s she began catching the eye of people beyond that sphere. Her work with the ACLU on gender discrimination earned her the beginnings of her reputation as a fierce advocate for women's rights. Her brief for *Reed v. Reed* in 1971 was a crucial factor in the Supreme Court's ruling to strike down an Idaho statute that declared men should be preferred to women when administering a deceased person's estate. However, as

Ruth Bader Ginsburg began to gain a reputation as a strong advocate for women's right in the 1970s.

much as Ginsburg wanted to argue that case before the Supreme Court, she was not chosen to do so. Her brief gained notice, though, even if Ginsburg wasn't the person arguing the case.

Breaking Boundaries: The Equal Protection Clause

It was no surprise that, after Ginsburg's success with gender discrimination work with the ACLU, doors finally began to open for her. In 1972, Columbia Law School finally offered Ginsburg tenure, making her the first tenured female faculty member in the institution's history. In 1973, the ACLU promoted Ginsburg from co-director of its Women's Rights Project to general counsel and member of the board of directors.

This finally gave Ginsburg her chance to argue before the Supreme Court. Over the course of the 1970s, she argued seven cases in front of the Supreme Court and won five of those. Her work mostly revolved around the equal protection clause of the Fourteenth Amendment of the United States Constitution.

The Fourteenth Amendment is considered one of the Reconstruction Amendments and was adopted as part of the Constitution on July 28, 1868. It was a response to slavery-related issues after the Civil War.

The amendment has five sections, but the most recognizable part is in Section 1:

No state shall make or enforce any law which shall abridge the privileges or immunities of citizens of the United States; nor shall any state deprive any person of life, liberty, or property, without due process of law; nor deny to any person within its jurisdiction the equal protection of the laws.[1]

The phrase "equal protection of the laws" has been frequently litigated in many landmark court cases, including *Brown v. Board of Education* (1954, about racial discrimination), *Roe v. Wade* (1973, about women's reproductive rights), *Reed v. Reed* (1971, the landmark case about gender discrimination that Ginsburg wrote a widely praised brief for), and more recently, *Bush v. Gore* (2000, about election recounts).

When the Supreme Court reviewed cases to determine whether laws violated the "equal protection of the laws" clause, it would apply three tests:

- Was there a rational basis for the law?

- Was the law substantially related to the achievement of an important government purpose?

- Did the law draw a distinction based on race, which is considered a suspect classification?

This legal precedent of examining laws on the basis of whether they drew a distinction based on race is where

Ginsburg found her opening to argue against gender discrimination in the 1970s. She argued that, like race, gender should be considered a "suspect classification." Thus, laws that discriminated based on gender should be subject to greater scrutiny.

At her confirmation hearings for her Supreme Court seat, Ginsburg explained the problem: While "race discrimination was immediately perceived as evil, odious, and intolerable," laws discriminating against women were not seen the same way.[2] Rather, they were seen as protecting women. Knowing that in the 1970s her audience in arguing these cases was mostly composed of men, Ginsburg wisely chose to argue cases that showed that gender discrimination was harmful to not only women but also men.

Of her work in the 1970s, she says:

Work [on gender discrimination] progressed on three fronts: We sought to advance, simultaneously, public understanding, legislative change, and change in judicial doctrine ... In one sense, our mission in the 1970s was easy: the targets were well defined. There was nothing subtle about the way things were. Statute books in the States and Nation were riddled with what we then called sex-based differentials.[3]

Interestingly, some of these "sex-based differentials" actually favored women. For example, in the early 1970s the Supreme Court reviewed a decision in a case that the ACLU had argued (and won) at the court of appeals level. In that case, the plaintiff, a man named Charles E. Moritz, challenged the Internal Revenue Service (**IRS**) about a tax code that said a single woman could claim a tax deduction for the cost of caring for an elderly, ailing dependent, but a single man could not.

Judges and legislators looked at cases like this and insisted that women actually had it good. There, specifically, they could claim a tax credit that men couldn't! In a larger sense, male judges and legislators looked at women's lives during that era as wide open and full of possibility. In a speech given at the University of Cape Town in South Africa in 2006, Ginsburg explained the sentiment of legislators and judges at the time:

Judges and legislators in the 1960s, and at least at the start of the 1970s, regarded differential treatment of men and women not as malign, but as operating benignly in women's favor. Legislators and judges, in those years, were overwhelmingly white, well-heeled, and male. Men holding elected and appointed offices generally considered themselves good husbands and fathers. Women, they thought, had the best of all possible worlds. Women could work if they wished; they could stay home if they chose. They could avoid jury duty if they were so inclined, or they could serve if they elected to do so. They could escape military duty or they could enlist.[4]

What those judges and legislators didn't recognize, however, was that even with more doors being open to women, double standards existed everywhere. For example, in some states, a woman could only work in a bar if that bar was owned by her husband or father. Women could serve in the military, but they weren't automatically entitled to the same housing and insurance benefits as men serving in the military. (Ginsburg challenged this in 1973's *Frontiero v. Richardson,* winning an 8–1 victory in the Supreme Court.) And in Iowa, families were allowed to stop supporting daughters once they turned eighteen but were required to support sons until they turned twenty-one.

Ginsburg believed in equality for everyone, and she fought for it—for everyone. During the 1970s, she fought numerous battles on behalf of women, but she also supported legal efforts to end unequal treatment for men. For example, one case that was near to her heart was a 1975 Supreme Court case about a **widower** named Stephen Wiesenfeld (*Weinberger v. Wiesenfeld*), who sought Social Security benefits so he could care for his newborn child after his wife died in childbirth. Wiesenfeld was denied the benefits because of his gender—women were entitled to them in similar situations, but not men. Ginsburg was delighted when Wiesenfeld won the case in a unanimous Supreme Court decision, saying, "Using sex as a convenient shorthand to substitute for financial need or willingness to bring up a baby did not comply with the equal protection principle, as the Court had grown to understand that principle."[5]

Ginsburg also challenged an Oklahoma law that allowed women to purchase a particular type of alcohol at age eighteen but required men to be twenty-one to buy that same alcohol. The law was based on the idea that men drink more and drive more than women and were thus more likely to commit alcohol-related offenses. Whether or not that was true, Ginsburg saw the inequality in the law as problematic and fought on behalf of the men in *Craig v. Boren* (1976).

In 1978, Ginsburg argued her last case as a lawyer in front of the Supreme Court, *Duren v. Missouri*, in which she argued that jury duty should be mandatory for women, just as it was for men. By making it voluntary, Ginsburg argued that it suggested a woman's service on a jury was less valuable than a man's. Once again, on the surface this looked like a law in favor of women—they didn't *have* to do jury duty. But Ginsburg looked beyond the surface and saw it for what it was: a double standard between the genders, which, in the grand scheme of things, set women apart from (and as less than) men.

To Ginsburg, in those 1970s court battles, it was all about establishing equality and eradicating the discrimination that people—mostly women—were facing in the legal system.

A Move to Washington

Ginsburg's work during the 1970s on gender discrimination didn't escape notice. On April 14, 1980, President Jimmy Carter appointed her to a seat on the US Court of Appeals for the District of Columbia Circuit.

This was a major step forward in Ginsburg's career. Her husband, Martin, a well-regarded expert in tax law, supported the move and took on a professorship at Georgetown University in Washington, DC, so the family could relocate. It was never a question: Martin was proud of his wife and supported her blossoming career. Martin said in an interview, "I have been supportive of my wife since the beginning of time, and she has been supportive of me. It's not sacrifice; it's family."[6]

Martin's support actually went beyond simply relocating. President Carter had already confirmed an appointment to a federal court in 1980 (which was an election year), and some Republican senators weren't pleased with the idea of confirming another Carter appointment during that same year. Martin spoke about the problem to his friend and client, business mogul (and later presidential candidate) Ross Perot, as well as to several other influential friends. Perot and the other friends called the senators to lobby on behalf of Ginsburg's appointment to the seat. In the end, only one senator on the Judiciary Committee voted against Ginsburg's nomination.

President Jimmy Carter appointed Ginsburg to the US Court of Appeals for the District of Columbia Circuit in 1980.

In addition, Martin sold all of his stock so that Ruth wouldn't be faced with removing herself from cases involving companies in which the family held financial interest. This also served to make the family's financial assets more transparent, which was critical when his wife faced nominations for high judicial positions.

Gaining a seat on the court of appeals was a big boost to Ginsburg's career—particularly since it was to the District of Columbia Circuit, which is thought to hear some of the most interesting cases in the nation. While Ginsburg is now viewed as part of the liberal wing of the court system, during the thirteen years she spent on the appeals court bench (1980 to 1993), she was viewed as rather moderate. Part of this is because she sometimes agreed with conservative colleagues such as Antonin Scalia. But part of it was also her strict adherence to gender equality, as opposed to specifically women's rights.

Feminist Backlash

Ginsburg wanted equal rights for women, but she didn't set out to give *more* rights to women than men. Rather, she wanted to see gender discrimination abolished and a true equality between the genders.

In the 1970s, Ginsburg had formed strong alliances and friendships with Gloria Steinem and other feminist icons. By the 1980s, Ginsburg found herself the target of some backlash from a new generation of feminists who felt that legislation should emphasize women's differences from men rather than focusing on their similarities. They saw Ginsburg's representation of male plaintiffs and her challenges of classifications that were problematic to men as well as women as the work of an "assimilationist." Catharine MacKinnon, a radical feminist and fellow lawyer, wrote, "As applied, the sameness standard has mostly gotten men the benefit of those few things women have historically had for all the good they did us."[7]

MacKinnon and other radical feminists of the time sought to target social structures that devalued women. In their efforts, they wanted to reinstate special protections for women that Ginsburg had opposed based on her belief that they supported gender discrimination, such as pornography bans and child-rearing benefits only for mothers. (Remember, Ginsburg had argued successfully that a man should be entitled to the same child-rearing benefits as a woman in *Weinberger v. Wiesenfeld*.)

Feminists such as MacKinnon viewed Ginsburg's nomination to the court of appeals with trepidation. They felt her advocacy for equal rights actually did more harm than good to the women's liberation movement.

Ginsburg disagreed with the feminists' negative views of her work. Of the claims of her being an assimilationist, she reminded people that "the litigation of the 1970s helped unsettle previously accepted conceptions of men's and women's separate spheres."[8] At a 1988 University of Chicago symposium on feminist legal thought of the 1970s, she also stated:

Different styles of feminist analysis undeniably produce conflicting responses in some contexts; but the common ground merits attention and statement in ways the wider public can understand. Each stand that will engage discussion and debate at this symposium probes and challenges facets of the traditional subordination of women. There is in this flourishing output, however, one discordant, jarring note—the tendency to regard one's feminism as the only true feminism, to denigrate rather than to appreciate the contributions of others. If that fatal tendency can be controlled, feminist legal theory, already an intellectual enterprise of the first dimension, will indeed be something to celebrate.[9]

Ginsburg disagreed that her work in gender equality had been a step backward for the feminist movement. Her approach had been different than that of Catharine MacKinnon and other feminists in the 1980s, but it was no less important. And if the two schools of feminism could work together, it would indeed be a step forward in women's rights in the legal sphere.

As it happened, Ginsburg would soon get a much larger audience to continue her work in gender equality when she was appointed to the United States Supreme Court.

An Unlikely Friendship

When Ginsburg took her seat on the US Court of Appeals, she made an unlikely friend in Justice Antonin Scalia (who later also sat on the Supreme Court with her). Although thought to be relatively moderate in her decisions while on the **appellate** court, Ginsburg was definitely a liberal at heart, and Scalia was a staunch conservative. The two weren't often on the same side of controversial issues, though Ginsburg did sometimes support Scalia's decisions. The two kept their disagreements on a professional level, however, and in their personal lives they were actually close friends.

When Scalia died in early 2016, Ginsburg wrote of him, "We were best buddies ... It was my great good fortune to have known him as a working colleague and a treasured friend."[10] The two famously shared a love of opera.

Their disagreements never intruded on their friendship. Nina Totenberg, a reporter for NPR, said of the two, "They liked to fight things out in good spirit—in fair spirit—not the way we see debates these days on television."[11] And Ginsburg felt that Scalia made her better. When he died, she wrote, "We disagreed now and then, but when I wrote for the court and received a Scalia dissent, the **opinion** ultimately released was notably better than my initial circulation. Justice Scalia nailed all the weak spots ... and gave me just what I needed to strengthen the majority opinion."[12]

Theirs was a true case of a beautiful friendship between two very different people who treasured what each brought to the table.

Judicial Structure in the United States

When considering Ruth Bader Ginsburg's rise in the United States judicial system, it's helpful to understand how that system is structured.

The highest court in the United States is the Supreme Court. This is where, at present day, Ruth Bader Ginsburg sits. It's a long road up to that prestigious seat, though.

Below the Supreme Court are thirteen appellate courts. These are all called US courts of appeals. The US Court of Appeals for the District of Columbia Circuit is where Ginsburg sat before her Supreme Court nomination and appointment. The US courts of appeals preside over ninety-four federal judicial districts that are organized into regional circuits (of which the District of Columbia Circuit is one). Each court hears challenges to district court decisions and is tasked with determining whether or not law was correctly applied in the court below it. The courts of appeals do not use a jury when hearing cases. Instead, they consist of a panel of three judges.

Below the courts of appeals are ninety-four district or trial courts. These are the courts we typically think of when we imagine a lawyer arguing a case in a court. These courts are presided over by a district judge, and the cases are heard by juries composed of twelve members. When a person is summoned for jury duty,

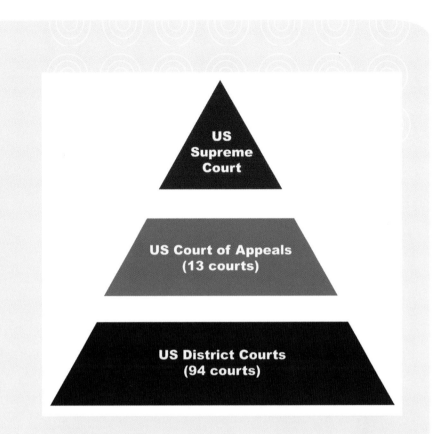

An illustration of the American judicial structure

they serve at a district or trial court that can be at a local/state or federal level. Each state in the US has at least one federal district court.

There are some other courts that branch off of this system, such as bankruptcy courts and Article I courts. But in general, the chain of command is district court, then court of appeals, then Supreme Court.

CHAPTER FOUR

A Move to the Supreme Court

Ruth Bader Ginsburg spent thirteen years on the United States Court of Appeals, from the confirmation of her appointment on June 18, 1980, up until 1993, when she was appointed to the Supreme Court. At that time, only one woman had ever sat on the Supreme Court: Justice Sandra Day O'Connor, who was appointed by President Ronald Reagan in 1981. O'Connor was the sole woman on the Supreme Court until President Bill Clinton nominated Ginsburg on June 14, 1993, and her appointment was confirmed by the United States Senate in August of that same year.

Ginsburg was sworn in as a Supreme Court justice on August 10, 1993.

A Tiny but Mighty Presence

Ginsburg is diminutive in stature, standing only 5 feet 1 inch (1.55 meters) tall and reportedly weighing just over 100 pounds (45 kilograms). But there is nothing tiny about her spirit. Even in her eighties, having survived two bouts of cancer (colon cancer in 1999 and pancreatic cancer in 2006) Ginsburg works out with a personal trainer and reportedly does twenty push-ups a day.

Ginsburg is known for not mincing words. Perhaps it is not surprising that in 1993, when President Bill Clinton wanted to fill Justice Byron White's vacant seat on the Supreme Court with someone who would bring a bit of diversity to the nearly all-male, all-Caucasian office, he thought of the tiny, feisty Ginsburg. She was not only female, but also Jewish. The Supreme Court hadn't had a Jewish justice since 1969, and it sorely lacked females.

But it shouldn't be assumed that Ginsburg was appointed simply because of the diversity she brought to the court. By this time, she was well known in Washington as a brilliant analyst and judge, and she was well regarded by her colleagues, both Democrats and Republicans.

In fact, Ginsburg was not President Clinton's initial choice for Justice White's seat. Clinton had thought to nominate Bruce Babbitt, a Democrat who had been a candidate for president in 1988 and had also been governor of Arizona. At the time, Babbitt was serving as Clinton's secretary of the interior. It was actually a Republican senator from Utah, Orrin Hatch, who suggested the liberal

Ginsburg (*far right*) is physically tiny compared to the other Supreme Court justices, but there's nothing tiny about her spirit and determination.

Ginsburg (along with Judge Stephen Breyer, another liberal US court of appeals judge). Hatch thought that Babbitt would be a tough sell with Republicans and even some Democrats, and he felt Ginsburg would be fairly easy to get confirmed. As Hatch described in his autobiography, "I knew them both and believed that, while liberal, they were highly honest and capable **jurists** and their confirmation would not embarrass the President. From my perspective, they were far better than the other likely candidates from a liberal Democrat administration."[1]

An Easy Sell

Senator Hatch was correct: Ginsburg was a relatively easy sell as a nominee to the Supreme Court. Although she was known for her work on gender discrimination and equal gender rights—typically liberal pursuits—she was overall considered relatively moderate, which made her

Women on the Bench

The United States' history of women in the legal profession dates back only about 150 years. While women may have acted in support positions in the legal profession before then, the first known woman admitted to the **bar** was Arabella Mansfield, who passed the Iowa bar in 1869 after studying for two years in her brother's law office. She did not have a formal law-school education, but that same year, Ada H. Kepley was the first woman in United States history to graduate from law school.

The next year, Esther Morris became the first woman in the United States to sit as a judge—she was appointed a justice of the peace in the Wyoming Territory. It wasn't until 1928 that a woman was appointed to a federal court—President Calvin Coolidge nominated Genevieve Cline to a seat on the US Customs Court that year, and Cline held that seat for twenty-five years.

The first woman to sit on the bench in a federal appeals court was Florence Allen, who took a seat on the United States Court of Appeals for the Sixth Circuit in 1934 after serving as a justice in Ohio's state supreme court.

While it's relatively common now to see women in high positions in the legal and judicial fields, the United States Supreme Court has remained largely dominated by men. As of 2016, of the 112 justices who have sat on the Supreme Court, only 4 have been women. That's just 3.5 percent!

The Supreme Court was established in 1789, but the first woman didn't join the court until almost two centuries later, when President Ronald Reagan appointed Sandra Day O'Connor to the court in 1981. O'Connor sat on the bench for twenty-five years, and before she retired, she was joined by the second woman to be appointed to the Supreme Court: Ruth Bader Ginsburg in 1993.

O'Connor retired in 2006 and Ginsburg was the sole women in the court until 2009, when she was joined by Sonia Sotomayor, the first Latina judge to be appointed to the court. A year later, Elena Kagan was appointed to the court as well. Both Sotomayor and Kagan were nominated by President Barack Obama.

There was one other female nominee to the Supreme Court, but she was not ultimately confirmed: Harriet Miers, who was nominated by President George W. Bush. Miers was not a popular nomination because she didn't have experience as a judge and her views were uncertain on some specific controversial issues. Having previous experience as a judge isn't a prerequisite for being confirmed as a United States Supreme Court justice, but most justices on the court have sat on the bench before being appointed.

an attractive choice for both Democrats and Republicans on the Senate Judiciary Committee.

Michael Comiskey, a professor of political science from Penn State, discussed Ginsburg's nomination in a 1994 issue of the journal *PS: Political Science and Politics*, saying:

> At least four factors pointed toward a smooth experience with the Judiciary Committee and a relatively easy confirmation. First were the nominee's outstanding credentials ... She was universally respected in the legal community for her intellect and her scholarly approach to cases. The American Bar Association's Standing Committee on the Federal Judiciary, which rates federal judicial nominees, gave her its highest rating: "well qualified." Second was her record ... on the federal Court of Appeals for the District of Columbia Circuit, as a "non-ideological moderate who eschews judicial activism." This reputation was fortified by her cordial relationships with both liberal and conservative judges and her often-expressed views on abortion rights with criticism of Roe v. Wade *as an overly activist decision that went too far too fast. Third, Ginsburg was a woman and, even more, a historic figure who had worked within the system for the steady achievement of legal equality for women ... Fourth, and largely as a result of the three previous factors, senators of both parties had told President Clinton that they would support Ginsburg's nomination.*[2]

Indeed, Comiskey and Hatch were correct: Ginsburg's confirmation process to the Supreme Court went relatively smoothly. Interestingly, just a few years before her nomination, Ginsburg had written about the process of testimony at judicial confirmation hearings, saying that judges must be impartial, so Supreme Court nominees should not tell senators how they would vote on any particular type of issue that might come before the Supreme Court. She maintained that potential justices must be evaluated on the basis of their previous judicial record.

During her confirmation hearings, Ginsburg held firm to this belief and refused to answer questions about issues such as the death penalty, citing it as an issue she might have to vote on if she were indeed confirmed to the Supreme Court. She did, however, speak freely about issues on which she had previously written briefs and opinions, such as gender equality.

In the end, Ginsburg was confirmed as the 107th justice of the Supreme Court in an almost unanimous vote: ninety-six members of the hundred-person Senate voted for her confirmation, and only three voted against it. (One member did not vote.) The three members of the committee who voted against Ginsburg were conservative Republicans. One of them, Senator Jesse Helms from North Carolina, cited her support of abortion rights as the reason he voted against her, saying he felt she was "likely to uphold the homosexual agenda."[3]

President Clinton was reportedly pleased with the confirmation and called her "a great Justice" who would "move the Court not left or right, but forward."[4]

Drama in the Committee

Why was an easy confirmation to the Supreme Court so important when Ginsburg was nominated? Partly because the Supreme Court had its fair share of drama in the late 1980s, and politicians in Washington were eager to avoid any further drama or scandal.

In 1987, President Ronald Reagan nominated Robert Bork, one of Ginsburg's fellow judges on the US Court of Appeals for the District of Columbia Circuit, to the Supreme Court. This nomination was wildly unpopular. Both civil rights and women's rights groups opposed his nomination because of his desire to roll back previous civil rights decisions and a fear that he would try to reverse the Supreme Court decision in *Roe v. Wade*. The ACLU publicly opposed Bork's nomination as well—he was one of only three nominees ever opposed by the organization. Many felt that Bork was an extremist who supported an unfair amount of power being given to the **executive branch** of the United States government. So controversial was Bork's nomination that there were even television commercials that portrayed Bork as an extremist, and Senator Ted Kennedy condemned Bork by stating, "Robert Bork's America is a land in which women would be forced into back-alley abortions, blacks would sit at segregated lunch counters, rogue police could break down citizens' doors in midnight raids, schoolchildren could not be taught about evolution, writers and artists could be censored at the whim of the government ..."[5] Bork claimed Kennedy's speech was inaccurate, and in reality Bork may have been right, but the damage to Bork's nomination was done, and the drama surrounding the nomination reached a fever pitch.

President George H. W. Bush nominated Clarence Thomas, also a judge (with Ginsburg) on the US Court of Appeals for the District of Columbia Circuit, to the Supreme Court in 1991, just a few years later, and that nomination also resulted in bitter arguments. President Bush had chosen Thomas for the seat when Justice Thurgood Marshall, the first African American justice on the Supreme Court, announced his retirement. Like Marshall, Thomas was African American and brought diversity to the mostly Caucasian bench. But Thomas was more conservative than Marshall, which appealed to President Bush. It did not necessarily appeal, however, to African American and civil rights organizations that feared Thomas's conservative leanings would set back the progress they had made during the civil rights era.

The controversy exploded when a law professor named Anita Hill came forward to report that Thomas had sexually harassed her when she had worked for him years before. Hill claimed that when she refused Thomas's invitations for a date, he harassed her by discussing pornography and sexual acts.

Whether Hill's accusations were true was never proven, and ultimately Thomas was confirmed to the Supreme Court. However, it was yet another embarrassment for the office, and it's no great surprise that after several years of drama surrounding Supreme Court nominees, President Clinton was keen to find a noncontroversial figure who would be easily confirmed by the Senate Judiciary Committee.

CHAPTER FIVE

On the Bench: Ruth Bader Ginsburg as Supreme Court Justice

R uth Bader Ginsburg's decades on the Supreme Court have been nothing if not eventful! She has been involved in numerous influential Supreme Court cases since taking her oath on August 10, 1993.

Ginsburg has long supported women's reproductive rights.

Ginsburg on Gender Equality

It's no surprise that Ginsburg has ruled on issues surrounding gender equality during her time on the bench. For one thing, even though the legal battle for gender equality started decades ago, it still rages on in the United States. There are still areas in which women are not granted equal rights to men, and women are still paid less than men on average. The Institute for Women's Policy Research states that in 2015 there was a "gender wage gap of 20 percent," with female workers in full-time positions making "only 80 cents for every dollar earned by men."[1] So while much progress has been made in gender equality, there is still work to be done.

Fairly early in her time on the bench, in 1996, Ginsburg presided over *United States v. Virginia*, a case challenging the Virginia Military Institute's (VMI) male-only admission policy as a violation of the Fourteenth Amendment's equal protection clause. In a 7–1 decision, the Supreme Court struck down VMI's admission policy.

As a member of the court, Ginsburg wrote for the majority in challenging the admission policy. The state of Virginia had suggested that instead of forcing VMI to admit women, a similar program to VMI's could be created for women (and would be known as the Virginia Women's Institute for Leadership, or VWIL). Ginsburg challenged this plan, saying, "The VWIL program is a pale shadow of VMI in terms of the range of curricular choices and faculty stature, funding, prestige, alumni

Ginsburg was instrumental in striking down the VMI policy that denied females admission to the institute.

support and influence."[2] Ginsburg went on to state, "Neither federal nor state government acts compatibly with equal protection when a law or official policy denies to women, simply because they are women, full citizenship stature—equal opportunity to aspire, achieve, participate in and contribute to society based on their individual talents and capacities."[3]

In other words, as she had successfully argued many times before, there was no justifiable reason for a woman to not be allowed the same rights as a man in this instance, and trying to establish such a reason was a clear violation of the equal protection clause of the Fourteenth

Amendment. Only this time, she was successfully challenging the long-held policy of a venerable institution that had been in existence since 1839.

Ginsburg on Equal Rights for Disabled Persons

Ginsburg not only believes in equal rights for both genders and for people of different racial backgrounds, she also believes in equal rights for the disabled. Ginsburg presented the court opinion for a landmark 1999 Supreme Court case, *Olmstead v. L. C.*, which some feel is one of the most important civil rights decision in United States history with regard to the lives of people with disabilities.

Up until about the 1960s, it was common practice for people with developmental or intellectual disabilities or certain types of mental illness to be housed in state-run institutions. Due to overcrowding and underfunding, these institutions became a nightmare for the people housed in them, who were often mistreated or malnourished. To correct this, in the 1960s there began a move toward **deinstitutionalization.**

But change is slow, and in the 1990s, when Lois Curtis (the L. C. in *Olmstead v. L. C.*) and Elaine Wilson, both from Georgia, were struggling with mental health problems and intellectual disabilities that rendered them unable to care for themselves, it was still not uncommon for people like Curtis and Wilson to be institutionalized.

In the case of both Curtis and Wilson, their doctors and teams at the institution would repeatedly discharge them, saying they were capable of living in the community *if properly supported*, but then they would not receive proper support, and so they would end up back in the institution.

This cycle happened over and over, with Curtis and Wilson not getting the community-based support that they were entitled to under the Americans with Disabilities Act (or **ADA**), a 1990 law that states, in part, that individuals with disabilities cannot be excluded from services due to their disability. The ADA also includes an "integration mandate" that states public agencies must "administer services, programs, and activities in the most integrated setting appropriate to the needs of the qualified individuals with disabilities."[4] And so, Sue Jamieson, an attorney for the Atlanta Legal Aid Society, filed a lawsuit on their behalf to help them get the supports they were entitled to. (The "Olmstead" in the case name comes from Tommy Olmstead, who was the commissioner of the Georgia Department of Human Resources at the time.)

The case went to the Supreme Court, where the state of Georgia argued that the appropriate supports were not provided to Curtis and Wilson due to a lack of funding, not because of their disability. Ginsburg found that under Title II of the ADA, "unnecessary institutional segregation … cannot be justified by lack of funding." She delivered the court's opinion that "states are required to place persons with mental disabilities in community settings rather than in institutions when the state's treatment professionals have determined that community placement is appropriate, the transfer from institutional care to a less restrictive setting is not opposed by the affected individual, and the placement can be reasonably accommodated."[5]

Because Curtis and Wilson's treatment professionals had deemed them capable of living in the community with appropriate support, that support had to be provided.

The *Olmstead* decision has been monumental in the fight for civil rights on behalf of people with disabilities. In 2009, the United States Justice Department made *Olmstead* a priority and began to enforce it in cases on the state level. The original *Olmstead* decision involved a psychiatric facility, but the decision is now being upheld with regard to all state- and Medicaid-funded institutions, such as nursing homes. In recent years, *Olmstead* has been applied in other contexts, such as the move to eliminate **sheltered workshops** for people with disabilities and the goal of providing **Medicaid waivers** to people with disabilities who would normally qualify for an institutional level of care.

It started as one small case on behalf of two women whose civil rights were being violated, but once it became a Supreme Court decision, this little case became a cornerstone for disability rights legislation.

Ginsburg on Abortion

Ginsburg has played a rather complicated role in the debate over abortion rights. In the broadest sense, she has strongly supported a women's right to choose abortion. But at the same time, she criticized the landmark *Roe v. Wade* decision, which has led some people to doubt her support of abortion rights.

It's important to understand that Ginsburg criticized the grounding behind the decision in *Roe v. Wade*, not the decision itself. She has always supported a woman's legal right to choose, but she felt that the *Roe v. Wade* decision was made based on an individual's right to privacy—that a woman and her doctor could consult and make the decision about an abortion. "The view you get," Ginsburg said, "is the tall doctor and the little woman who needs him."[6] In other words, women were still not being treated as equals, which is where the problem in the decision lay, in Ginsburg's mind.

Instead, Ginsburg felt the decision should have been based on the equal protection clause of the Fourteenth Amendment. Constitutional law professor Sonja West summed up Ginsburg's position in a 2016 *Washington Post* article:

> *The key to understanding Justice Ginsburg's views on the constitutional right to abortion is that she sees it as a question of equal protection and not of privacy ... She has said on many occasions that for women to attain true equality with men, they must have sole control over their fertility. This control, in [her] view, is tied to a woman's ability to be independent, which is in turn tied to her status as an equal citizen.[7]*

This belief about the foundation behind *Roe v. Wade* is part of what led to Ginsburg's dissent in a 2007 Supreme Court case, *Gonzales v. Carhart*. The case revolved around the Partial-Birth Abortion Ban Act of 2003, which prohibits a type of late-term abortion called "intact dilation and extraction." In its most basic terms, this type of abortion involves the fetus's life being terminated when part of its body is outside of the mother's body, and it usually occurs sometime after about the fifteenth week of pregnancy, though the actual **gestation** is not specified in the law.

Dr. LeRoy Carhart, a doctor who performed late-term abortions, wanted the Partial-Birth Abortion Ban Act struck down, and Attorney General Alberto Gonzales, on behalf of the government, argued that the law should be upheld. The Supreme Court ultimately decided to uphold the ban on late-term abortions, but Ginsburg dissented.

Part of her argument was that the law had no exception written to provide for the health of the mother. That is, if a late-term abortion were deemed medically necessary to preserve the health of the mother, it could not be done because the Partial-Birth Abortion Ban Act did not allow for it. In her dissent, she commented, "The court deprives women of the right to make an autonomous choice, even at the expense of their safety. This way of thinking reflects ancient notions about women's place in the family and under the Constitution— ideas that have long since been discredited."[8]

Another part of Ginsburg's dissent had to do with her staunch belief that for a woman to have true equality, she needed to be able to make her own life decisions. She wrote, "The Act, and the court's defense of it, cannot be understood as anything other than an effort to chip away at a right declared again and again by this court—and with increasing comprehension of its centrality to women's lives."[9]

In 2016, Ginsburg was again part of an abortion discussion at the Supreme Court level when she was part of *Whole Woman's Health v. Hellerstedt* (informally known as the "Texas abortion clinics case"). In that case, abortion providers challenged a Texas law that required physicians who perform abortions to have admitting privileges at a nearby hospital and that required abortion clinics to have facilities comparable to an ambulatory surgical center. Ginsburg supported the court's decision to reverse the law on the grounds that the law made it difficult for a woman to obtain an abortion in Texas and thus was a violation of a woman's constitutional rights to seek an abortion.

On the surface, the law seems reasonable: Texas legislators ostensibly wanted safer facilities and conditions for women to have abortions. But the problem behind the law was that if enacted, it would reduce the number of abortion clinics in Texas from more than forty to roughly ten. More than thirty of the currently operating clinics could not meet the requirements of the Texas law and thus would have to close.

Ginsburg's concern was that the closure of so many of the state's abortion clinics would mean women wanting an abortion would turn to unsafe, back-alley abortion clinics, as they had in the days before *Roe v. Wade*. In her concurring opinion for the court, Ginsburg wrote, "When a State severely limits access to safe and legal procedures, women in desperate circumstances may resort to unlicensed rogue practitioners, **faute de mieux**, at great risk to their health and safety." She also cited the fact that numerous other more dangerous medical procedures than abortion (including childbirth) were "not subject to ambulatory surgical-center or hospital admitting-privileges requirements."[10] Indeed, medical research backs up Ginsburg's claim, showing that roughly 1 in every 11,000 women died in childbirth between 1998 and 2006, but only 1 in every 167,000 women died from complications of abortion.[11]

Even if Ginsburg's original dedication to upholding women's abortion rights was questioned by some, her decisions on the topic while on the Supreme Court indicate that she is indeed a staunch supporter of abortion rights.

Ginsburg on Marriage Equality

Marriage equality has been a hot and controversial topic while Ginsburg has been on the Supreme Court. It's a topic that has been brewing for years and has in recent years seen considerable movement.

Back in 1972, the Supreme Court dismissed the case of *Baker v. Nelson*, in which a male same-sex couple tried to gain the right to legally marry. The next year, Maryland became the first state to ban same-sex marriage. This set up the status quo for the better part of two decades. While same-sex couples were gradually becoming more accepted by society, these couples were still denied the legal right to marry.

Then, in 1993, the Hawaii Supreme Court ruled that denying same-sex couples the right to marry was a violation of the equal protection clause of the Fourteenth Amendment. This started a slow chain of events that has led up to recent Supreme Court involvement in the issue. One key event was President Clinton signing the Defense of Marriage Act (a federal law) in 1996, which denied federal benefits to married same-sex couples.

In the late 1990s and early 2000s, states began passing domestic partnership statutes, and civil unions became legal for same-sex couples in certain states. In 2003, the Massachusetts Supreme Court legalized same-sex marriage, but shortly thereafter, eleven other states passed amendments banning same-sex marriage. And so it went, with states having the authority to allow or deny same-sex marriage. A same-sex couple could travel to another state to get married, but if their residence wasn't in a state that allowed same-sex marriage, the union wouldn't be recognized as valid in a legal sense.

In 2010, same-sex couples got a major victory when a United States district court judge, Joseph Tauro, ruled that a portion of the Defense of Marriage Act was unconstitutional. In 2011, the Obama administration announced that it would no longer defend the Defense of Marriage Act. President Obama went a step further in 2012, when he became the first president in office to openly express support for same-sex marriage.

Over the next several years, a number of cases made their way to the Supreme Court, including a challenge to the Defense of Marriage Act (*United States v. Windsor*) and numerous challenges to state-level bans on same-sex marriage. In 2015, the Supreme Court heard the case of *Obergefell v. Hodges*, which was a group of six consolidated cases against same-sex marriage bans in four states (Ohio, Michigan, Tennessee, and Kentucky).

Obergefell v. Hodges was decided on June 26, 2015, a landmark win for the LGBTQ community. In a 5–4 decision, the Supreme Court found that same-sex couples were entitled to the fundamental right to marry based on the Fourteenth Amendment—specifically, the equal protection clause and the due process clause (which safeguards citizens from being denied life, liberty, or property). Because of *Obergefell v. Hodges*, all states must issue marriage licenses to same-sex couples and must recognize same-sex marriages, even if they were performed in other jurisdictions.

Ginsburg did not write the final decision in *Obergefell v. Hodges*, but she openly supported it—while admitting that if she had written it, she would have focused more on the equal protection aspect of it. When speaking of the decision, she referred to a 1981 case (*Kirchberg v. Feenstra*) which resulted in Louisiana's "head and master rule" finally being struck down. The head and master rule essentially established the husband as the head and master of a household, with his wife subordinate to him.

When oral arguments for *Obergefell v. Hodges* were heard in the Supreme Court, the attorney for the state of Michigan argued that marriage was defined as one man and one woman and had been so for thousands of years. Ginsburg replied:

> *We have changed our idea about marriage. Marriage today is not what it was under the common law tradition, under the civil law tradition. Marriage was a relationship of a dominant male to a subordinate female. That ended as a result of this court's decision in 1982 when Louisiana's Head and Master Rule was struck down. And no state was allowed to have such a marriage anymore.*[12]

Ginsburg argued that if we had changed our definition of marriage to make it a more **egalitarian** institution for men and women, then by the same token, the definition of marriage should be altered to be free of gender stereotypes. Ginsburg has long been known as a believer of a "living" Constitution—that is, a document that changes and evolves as times change, and that can be reinterpreted by judges based on changes in society. Whereas the **Founding Fathers** may have conceived of marriage as involving one

Ginsburg has been a vocal supporter for marriage equality, even though she didn't author the decision in *Obergefell v. Hodges*.

man and one woman, justices like Ginsburg believe that the Founders' original intent should be reevaluated and updated based on a changing society over time.

When the case was being heard before the Supreme Court, Ginsburg used wit and wisdom to effectively shut down arguments against legalizing same-sex marriage. One lawyer arguing for keeping same-sex marriage bans tried to argue that marriage is about **procreation** and thus should not apply to same-sex couples. Ginsburg quickly answered, "Suppose a couple, 70-year-old couple, comes in and they want to get married? You don't have to ask them any questions. You know they are not going to have any children."[13] And when faced with arguments that allowing same-sex marriage would weaken the overall institution of marriage, Ginsburg pointed out, "All of the incentives, all of the benefits that marriage affords would still be available. So you're not taking away anything from heterosexual couples. They would have the very same incentive to marry, all the benefits that come with marriage that they do now."[14] Even though Ginsburg didn't write the opinion on the *Obergefell v. Hodges* case, her support for it comes as no surprise—she has long supported LGBTQ equality and has spoken frankly about it. Before the case, she spoke to Greg Stohr and Matthew Winkler of Bloomberg and stated:

The change in people's attitudes on that issue has been enormous. In recent years, people have said, "This is the way I am." And others looked around, and we discovered it's our next-door neighbor—we're very fond of them. Or it's our child's best friend, or even our child. I think that as more and more people came out and said that "this is who I am," the rest of us recognized that they are one of us.[15]

It might surprise some that a woman married to the same man for fifty-six years, until his death, would be such a staunch supporter of same-sex marriage. But it really shouldn't surprise anyone, given Ginsburg's lifelong commitment to ensuring equality and upholding the Fourteenth Amendment's equal protection clause.

Personal Challenges While on the Bench

Sitting on the Supreme Court of the United States would be a massive undertaking for anyone, but Ginsburg's personal life has undergone some upheaval during her Supreme Court tenure.

In 1999, she was diagnosed with colon cancer, which required surgery and then chemotherapy and radiation. Despite the grueling treatment, she didn't miss a single day of work.

A decade later, in early 2009, Ginsburg was diagnosed with pancreatic cancer and underwent surgery. This time, she missed work—but only for ten days. The fact that she made a full recovery is nothing short of extraordinary. Pancreatic cancer is the fourth-deadliest form of cancer, and 95 percent of patients with it die within five years. The odds are slightly better for people whose cancer is detected early, as Ginsburg's was, but the outlook is still quite grim. Very few people survive it long term, and yet somehow Ginsburg has managed to.

Heartbreak struck Ruth in June 2010, when her beloved husband, Martin, who had beaten testicular cancer early in their marriage, ultimately succumbed to metastatic cancer just four days after their fifty-sixth wedding anniversary. The man who Ruth had described as "always my best friend" had gone but had left her with decades of memories and two children. Their children, Jane and James, urged Ruth to go to court the day after Martin died, as she had an opinion in a key case—one in which a Christian group was trying to ban LGBTQ students from attending meetings at a public university. And so she went and sat in court, with a dark ribbon in her hair as a tribute to her love and life partner.

CHAPTER SIX

The Future

Although Ruth Bader Ginsburg is now in her eighties, an age at which most people would expect her to slow down, she shows few signs of doing so. Her long-term goals remain a focus of her work— a career she doesn't seem poised to give up anytime soon.

Emphasis on Foreign Law

Early in the 1960s, when her career was in its infancy, Ginsburg participated in the Project on International Procedure, a brainchild of Columbia Law School. The project invited American lawyers "to compare civil procedure in representative European countries."[1] Ginsburg's part of the project involved coauthoring a book on civil procedure in Sweden, including judicial

One of *Glamour* magazine's Women of the Year in 2012

organization and the entire process of trying and ultimately deciding a civil case. Ginsburg found herself fascinated by Sweden's legal proceedings and, perhaps even more so, the fact that women had many more opportunities in the legal profession in Sweden than they did in the United States.

That experience has stayed with Ginsburg throughout her long and distinguished legal career. Debates still exist about whether foreign law should be considered when deciding cases in the United States, and Ginsburg has been fairly outspoken about her belief that it is reasonable to cite foreign law in deciding American constitutional cases.

Some of the more conservative justices on the Supreme Court, including John G. Roberts Jr., Samuel A. Alito Jr., Clarence Thomas, and before his death, Antonin Scalia, disagree with Ginsburg's view and feel that foreign law should *not* be cited in United States constitutional cases. Opponents such as these justices worry that relying on a foreign judge's decision in a case that will shape constitutional law is dangerous from an accountability standpoint. In the United States, people elect politicians, so in theory senators (who are responsible for confirming Supreme Court justices) and other politicians are accountable to their constituents. A judge in a foreign country, they argue, really has no accountability to the American people and thus should not be influential in shaping constitutional law.

In a 2009 interview, Ginsburg remarked:

> *I frankly don't understand all the brouhaha lately from Congress and even from some of my colleagues about referring to foreign law … Why shouldn't we look to the wisdom of a judge from abroad with at least as much ease as we would read a law review article written by a professor?*[2]

Ginsburg's argument was based on her belief that citing foreign precedent in a legal judgment did *not* mean a United States court was bound to foreign law; rather, it meant the United States court was examining the reasoning in another country's legal decision and considering it when making its own.

Interestingly, while Ginsburg adamantly believes in the United States Constitution as a living document that should be reviewed, revised, and reinterpreted in light of changing times, she went back to the Founding Fathers to support her belief in foreign and international law when she gave a 2010 speech at the International Academy of Comparative Law at American University, saying:

> *From the birth of the United States as a nation, foreign and international law influenced legal reasoning and judicial decision-making. Founding fathers, most notably Alexander Hamilton and John Adams, were familiar with leading international law treatises, the law merchant, and English constitutional law. And they used that learning as advocates in legal contests.*[3]

She also cited Chief Justice John Marshall (the fourth chief justice of the Supreme Court, who served from 1801 to 1835), who said that "the law of nations … is part of the law of our land. Decisions of the courts of other countries … show how the law of nations is understood elsewhere, and will be considered in determining the rule which is to prevail here."[4]

Quite simply and plainly, Ginsburg stated her views on citing international and foreign law as this: "The US judicial system will be the poorer … if we do not both share our experience with, and learn from, legal systems with values and a commitment to democracy similar to our own."[5]

It's a somewhat contentious topic, but Ginsburg has never been known to shy away from such things.

The Continuing Battle Against Gender Discrimination

Ginsburg's entry into the public eye really began when she became known for her work on gender discrimination cases, and that continues to be one of her focuses. Her stance is that "gender lines in the law are bad for everyone: bad for women, bad for men, and bad for children." And indeed, while she was seen by many as a champion for women's rights, much of her work actually focused on cases that involved discrimination against men because, as she put it, "discrimination against males operates against females as well."[6]

In recent years, Ginsburg has continued to work on cases related to gender discrimination—sometimes directly, and sometimes tangentially. In her mind, things like abortion rights and marriage rights are all tied up with gender equality. Stripping a woman of her reproductive rights, Ginsburg believes, is a form of gender discrimination. Not allowing same-sex couples to marry is also a form of gender discrimination. Ginsburg frequently cites the equal protection clause of the Fourteenth Amendment when arguing for gender equality, and her fight against gender discrimination continues to this day.

For example, in 2014 Ginsburg wrote a scathing dissent against the Supreme Court's ruling that for-profit businesses could be exempt from a law based on the company's religious beliefs. In that particular case, *Burwell v. Hobby Lobby Stores, Inc.*, Hobby Lobby filed a suit to allow them to be exempt from a law under the Affordable Care Act that said employers must provide female employees with contraceptives. The owners of Hobby Lobby are evangelical Christians who believe that life begins at conception, and in their religious view, certain types of contraceptives (including so-called morning-after pills and **IUDs**) that prevent a fertilized egg from implanting are essentially tools of abortion. Due to their religious beliefs, the owners of Hobby Lobby did not wish to provide these contraceptives to their female employees.

The case made its way up through the court system and ultimately into the Supreme Court, where the court

Ginsburg on the occasion of her twentieth year on the Supreme Court bench, in 2013

majority ruled in favor of Hobby Lobby on the basis that the company was protected under the 1993 Religious Freedom Restoration Act. Ginsburg wrote a thirty-five-page dissent against the court's ruling, stating that "the exemption sought by Hobby Lobby would … deny legions of women who do not hold their employers' beliefs access to contraceptive coverage." She went on to suggest that the Affordable Care Act's provision for birth control was not an example of government coercion (as some pro-life persons and organizations felt), but rather was designed to allow women to make their own reproductive choices:

> *Any decision to use contraceptives made by a woman covered under Hobby Lobby's ... plan will not be propelled by the Government, it will be the woman's autonomous choice, informed by the physician she consults.*[7]

Ginsburg's ultimate point, in her blistering dissent, was that religious rights should not trump individual rights. In the case of contraceptives, she was concerned about women's rights being set aside, but in her dissent she wondered about the larger message the court's decision would send.

> *Would the exemption ... extend to employers with religiously grounded objections to blood transfusions (Jehovah's Witnesses); antidepressants (Scientologists); medications derived from pigs, including anesthesia, intravenous fluids, and pills coated with gelatin (certain Muslims, Jews, and Hindus); and vaccinations (Christian Scientists, among others)?*[8]

Ultimately, Ginsburg's dissent was so widely read and well regarded among supporters of individual and women's reproductive rights that a musician even set portions of it to music!

In a similar vein, Ginsburg supported the 2015 *Obergefell v. Hodges* decision that legalized same-sex marriage, and she supported abortion rights in the 2016 *Whole Woman's Health v. Hellerstedt* ruling. It's clear from her activity in the court that her determination to further gender equality in the legal system hasn't changed.

In a 2015 interview with Bloomberg, Ginsburg said, "I was a law school teacher. And that's how I regard my role here with my colleagues [in the Supreme Court], who haven't had the experience of growing up female and don't fully appreciate the arbitrary barriers that have been put in women's way."[9] Ginsburg cites what she says is an "unconscious bias" that still exists against women in the United States and continues to challenge that bias.

Awards and Accolades

With a career as distinguished as Ginsburg's, it's not surprising that accolades and awards would follow. She started out by earning New York State Regents and Cornell scholarships and then graduating with high honors from Cornell University. She then won coveted positions on both the *Harvard Law Review* and *Columbia Law Review*. In 1977, she was selected by *Time* as one of ten outstanding United States law school professors. In 1979, she was awarded the Society of American Law Teachers annual Outstanding Teacher of Law Award. In 1980, she won Barnard College's annual Woman of Achievement Award. In 1997, she received the first Sophia Smith Award from Smith College.

She has received numerous honorary degrees as well. Lewis and Clark College, Amherst College, Rutgers University, Hebrew Union College, Brooklyn Law School,

Georgetown University Law Center, Vermont Law School, and American University have all awarded her honorary degrees. In 2009, Willamette University awarded her an honorary doctor of laws degree, and Princeton University followed suit in 2010. Harvard, one of her alma maters, followed up in 2011 with the same honorary degree. In 2015, Radcliffe University awarded her the Radcliffe Medal.

Around that same time, she achieved recognition from *Forbes* magazine, when they named her number forty-eight of the One Hundred Most Powerful Women. (She beat out her fellow female Supreme Court justice Sonia Sotomayor, who came in fifty-fifth.) Similarly, she was named one of *Time* magazine's One Hundred Most Influential People in 2015. And *Glamour* magazine named her a Woman of the Year in 2012. She's also a popular figure on *Saturday Night Live*, where she has been portrayed by comedian Kate McKinnon.

In 2013, Ginsburg was awarded the American Association of Law School's Section on Women in Legal Education Lifetime Achievement Award. The Section on Women in Legal Education has more than 1,500 members and is the largest organization of female law faculty in the United States. Ginsburg was the first recipient of the award—a great honor. Danne Johnon, the chair of the Section on Women in Legal Education when the award was established, described Ginsburg as an obvious choice for the award, saying, "Justice Ginsburg is a rock star in our world."[10]

Retirement

Although she has reached the age by which many would have long since retired, Ginsburg has no plans to do so. When Justice John Paul Stevens retired from the Supreme Court in 2010, Ginsburg became the senior member of the court's liberal wing, which puts her in a powerful position. It isn't one she plans to give up anytime soon, even while critics point to her age as a reason why she should retire. "I happen to be the oldest [justice on the Supreme Court]," she commented in a 2015 interview, "but John Paul Stevens didn't step down until he was 90."[11]

Ginsburg's fitness to serve on the Supreme Court has also been questioned. She has famously been caught napping at two State of the Union addresses (2010 and 2015) and a presidential address to a joint session of Congress in 2013. Ginsburg shrugged it off and blamed it on the wine she'd had for dinner before the 2015 event: "I was not 100 percent sober … I vowed this year just sparkling water—stay away from the wine—but the dinner was so delicious it needed wine." Reportedly, Justice Anthony Kennedy had brought "very fine California wine" to the dinner, so Ginsburg decided to indulge in a glass—and promptly fell asleep during the president's address later that night![12] At least the president is in good company—Ginsburg reportedly dozed off during Pope Francis's historic 2015 address to Congress as well. Her "power naps" during these events have in fact become something of a joke on Twitter.

Recognized Where It All Began

In addition to receiving honorary degrees and awards, Ginsburg has been honored in another, rather unique way. The New York City Bar Association created the Justice Ruth Bader Ginsburg Distinguished Lecture on Women and the Law in 2000 to recognize Ginsburg's many achievements and her contributions to advancements in women's rights. Each year, a different woman delivers the lecture. Past lectures have been given by former Secretary of State Madeleine K. Albright (2001), Supreme Court Justice Elena Kagan (2014), and Ginsburg's old friend, feminist icon Gloria Steinem (2015).

In 2016, Ginsburg went head to head with presidential candidate Donald Trump, commenting, "I can't imagine what the country would be … with Donald Trump as our president." She later added, "He is a faker. He has no consistency about him. He says whatever comes into his head at the moment. He really has an ego." Trump turned to Twitter and responded, "Justice Ginsburg of the U.S. Supreme Court has embarrassed all by making very dumb political statements about me. Her mind is shot—resign!"[13]

Days later, Ginsburg apologized for her remarks—though she stopped short of saying her opinions had in any way changed. She simply expressed regret for having shared her views on the presidential candidate, saying, "Judges should avoid commenting on a candidate for public office ... In the future I will be more circumspect."[14]

Still, Ginsburg has not expressed that there is any validity to suggestions that she should consider retiring. Part of the retirement talk is political posturing. In 2011, Harvard Law professor Randall Kennedy wrote an essay suggesting that both Justices Ginsburg and Breyer (also on the liberal wing) should retire while Barack Obama was still in office, so that a Democratic president would be in office to nominate their replacements.

It's a logical political move, but one that Ginsburg dismissed, saying, "And who do you think Obama could have nominated and got confirmed that you'd rather see on a court?"[15] Given the Republican-controlled Senate, this was a valid concern. The Senate was seen as likely to block any liberal nomination from President Obama. Indeed, in 2016 the Senate refused to act on Obama's nomination of Merrick Garland—viewed by many as a relatively uncontroversial, moderate choice—to fill Antonin Scalia's seat on the court.

Supreme Court appointments last until retirement or death, so it's unlikely that Ginsburg will be leaving the bench anytime soon. The fact that she recently hired the four Supreme Court clerks who will assist her through 2018 is a good indicator that she doesn't plan to retire. The tiny, frail-appearing Ginsburg seems to have nine lives, having already successfully battled two serious bouts of cancer—one of them almost always fatal.

Despite being the oldest justice on the Supreme Court, Ginsburg has no plans to step down.

The Legacy of the Notorious R.B.G.

It's not often that a Supreme Court justice achieves rock-star status among the young demographic, but Ginsburg has done just that. Her work inspired a law student at New York University named Shana Knizhnik to create a Tumblr blog dedicated to "the Notorious R.B.G." The site proved wildly popular and has fifty-five thousand followers—one of whom is Ginsburg herself. "I think it's amusing. It's quite well done. There are some serious things on it. There are some funny things," Ginsburg said of the site.[16]

Future Women on the Bench

Now that four women have served on the United States Supreme Court, undoubtedly there will be more women holding that position in the future. With the passing of Justice Antonin Scalia in February 2016, a vacancy opened up on the bench. President Barack Obama nominated Judge Merrick Garland for the seat, but the Senate refused to consider the nomination, saying that because it was Obama's last year in office, the nomination should wait for the next president. This is largely because the Republican Senate hoped that the justice would be nominated by a Republican president who would prefer a more conservative judge.

Other candidates whom the Obama administration reportedly considered for Scalia's seat included two other men and two women: Judge Jane L. Kelly and Judge Ketanji Brown Jackson. Kelly is currently a judge on the United States Court of Appeals for the Eighth Circuit, while Jackson is a judge for the United States District Court for the District of Columbia. Had Jackson been the nominee and been confirmed, she would have been the first African American woman to sit on the United States Supreme Court.

In February 2017, President Donald Trump nominated Neil Gorsuch, a judge on the United States Court of Appeals for the Tenth Circuit, to fill Justice Scalia's seat.

The name of the site is a play on the name of the rapper Notorious B.I.G., and it features not only blog posts but also T-shirts, which Ginsburg has reportedly given out as gifts. The site has also spawned a book, *Notorious RBG: The Life and Times of Ruth Bader Ginsburg*, written by Knizhnik and fellow Ginsburg enthusiast Irin Carmon. Carmon says of Ginsburg:

The kind of raw excitement that surrounds her is palpable. There's a counterintuitiveness. We have a particular vision of someone who's a badass—a 350-pound rapper. And she's this tiny Jewish grandmother. She doesn't look like our vision of power, but she's so formidable, so unapologetic, and a survivor in every sense of the word.[17]

One thing is for certain: the Notorious R.B.G. certainly isn't boring. And with a reputation like hers, she won't likely be forgotten anytime soon.

1933

Ruth Jane Bader is born in Brooklyn, New York.

1959

Graduates from Columbia Law School and begins clerking for Judge Palmieri of the US District Court for the Southern District of New York.

1972

Becomes the first tenured female professor at Columbia Law School and cofounds the Women's Rights Project for the ACLU.

1955

Gives birth to daughter Jane.

1965

Gives birth to son James.

Begins studies at Harvard Law School.

1956

Authors first Supreme Court brief (*Reed v. Reed*).

1971

Graduates from Cornell University and marries Martin Ginsburg.

1954

Begins teaching at Rutgers University.

1963

Appointed to US Court of Appeals for the District of Columbia by President Jimmy Carter.

1980

1999

Presents Supreme Court opinion for landmark *Olmstead v. L. C.* case. Also successfully battles colon cancer without missing a day of work.

1993

Appointed to US Supreme Court by President Bill Clinton.

2010

Loses husband Martin Ginsburg to cancer.

2015

Votes to legalize same-sex marriage in *Obergefell v. Hodges.*

Writes Supreme Court's decision in landmark *United States v. Virginia* case.

1996

Writes scathing dissent in Supreme Court's *Burwell v. Hobby Lobby Stores, Inc.*, a case that attempted to limit women's reproductive rights based on a company's religious beliefs.

2014

Successfully battles pancreatic cancer despite only a 5 percent chance of long-term survival for that type of cancer.

2009

Supports Supreme Court's decision to reverse Texas law that made it difficult for women to obtain abortions in *Whole Woman's Health v. Hellerstedt.*

2016

SOURCE NOTES

Chapter 1

1. James Roland, *Ruth Bader Ginsburg: Iconic Supreme Court Justice* (Minneapolis, MN: Lerner, 2016).

2. Elinor Porter Swiger, *Women Lawyers at Work* (Winter Haven, FL: Messner, 1978).

3. *Hearings Before the Committee on the Judiciary, United States Senate, on the Nomination of Ruth Bader Ginsburg, to Be Associate Justice of the Supreme Court of the United States*, 103rd Congress (July 20-23, 1993).

4. Ruth Bader Ginsburg, "US Supreme Court Justice Nomination Acceptance Address," Speech delivered June 14, 1993, American Rhetoric Online Speech Bank, http://www.americanretoric.com/speeches/ruthbaderginsburgusscnominationspeech.htm.

5. Philip Galanes, "Ruth Bader Ginsburg and Gloria Steinem on the Unending Fight for Women's Rights," *New York Times*, November 14, 2015, http://www.nytimes.com/2015/11/15/fashion/ruth-bader-ginsburg-and-gloria-steinem-on-the-unendng-fight-for-womens-rights.html?_r=1.

6. Ibid.

7. Ibid.

Chapter 2

1. "Tribute: The Legacy of Ruth Bader Ginsburg and WRP Staff," ACLU, https://www.aclu.org/other/tribute-legacy-ruth-bader-ginsburg-and-wrp-staff.

2. "A Brief Biography of Justice Ginsburg," Columbia Law School, http://www.law.columbia.edu/law_school/communications/reports/winter2004/bio.

3. Galanes, "Ruth Bader Ginsburg and Gloria Steinem on the Unending Fight for Women's Rights."

4. Irin Carmon and Shana Knizhnik, "'Marty Was Always My Best Friend': Ruth Bader Ginsburg's Love Story." *Jezebel*, October 27, 2015, http://jezebel.com/marty- was-always-my-best-friend-ruth-bader-ginsburgs-l-1738733789.

5. Ibid.

6. Roya Rafei, "Ruth Bader Ginsburg: The Former Rutgers Law Professor Led the Legal Campaign for Gender Equality," *Rutgers Today*, February 29, 2016, http://news.rutgers.edu/feature/ruth-bader-ginsburg-former-rutgers-law-professor-led-legal-campaign-gender-equality/20160228#.V-Wk7DKZPm0.

7. Kenneth M. Davidson, Ruth Bader Ginsburg, and Herma H. Kay, *Sex-Based Discrimination: Text, Case, and Materials* (St. Paul, MN: West Publishing Co., 1974) xii-xiii.

8. Alli Maloney, "Five Best Revelations from Gloria Steinem and RBG's Lunch Date," *New York Times*, November 16, 2015, http://nytlive.nytimes.com/womenintheworld/2015/11/16/5-best-revelations-from-gloria-steinem-and-rbgs-lunch-date.

9. Ibid.

10. Rafei, "Ruth Bader Ginsburg."

11. Maloney, "Five Best Revelations from Gloria Steinem and RBG's Lunch Date."

Chapter 3

1. Editors of the Encyclopedia Britannica, "Fourteenth Amendment," *Encyclopedia Britannica*, Accessed November

17, 2016, https://www.britannica.com/topic/Fourteenth-Amendment.

2. Neil A. Lewis, "Ginsburg Promises Judicial Restrain if She Joins Court," *New York Times*, July 21, 1993, http://www.nytimes.com/1993/07/21/us/the-supreme-court-ginsburg-promises-judicial-restraint-if-she-joins-court.html.

3. Ruth Bader Ginsburg, "Advocating the Elimination of Gender-Based Discrimination: The 1970s New Look at the Equality Principle," Speech delivered at the University of Cape Town, South Africa, February 10, 2006, https://www.supremecourt.gov/publicinfo/speeches/sp_02-10-06.html.

4. Ibid.

5. Ibid.

6. Stephen Labaton, "The Man Behind the High Court Nominee," *New York Times*, June 17, 1993, http://www.nytimes.com/1993/06/17/us/the-man-behind-the-high-court-nominee.html?pagewanted=all.

7. Jeffrey Rosen, "The Book of Ruth," *New Republic*, August 1, 1993, https://newrepublic.com/article/61837/the-book-ruth.

8. Ibid.

9. Ruth Bader Ginsburg, "Some Reflections on the Feminist Legal Thought of the 1970s," *University of Chicago Legal Forum* no. 1 (1989), http://chicagounbound.uchicago.edu/cgi/viewcontent.cgi?article=1047&context=uclf.

10. "Ginsburg and Scalia: 'Best Buddies,'" NPR, February 15, 2016, http://www.npr.org/2016/02/15/466848775/scalia-ginsburg-opera-commemorates-sparring-supreme-court-friendship.

11. Ibid.

12. Robert Barnes, "How the Other Justices Remember Antonin Scalia," *Washington Post*, February 14, 2016, https://www.washingtonpost.com/politics/courts_law/how-the-other-

justices-remember-antonin-scalia/2016/02/14/30a53ae4-
d34b-11e5-9823-02b905009f99_story.html.

Chapter 4

1. Orrin Hatch, *Square Peg: Confessions of a Citizen-Senator*
    (New York: Basic Books, 2003).

2. Michael Comiskey, "The Usefulness of Senate Confirmation
    Hearings for Judicial Nominees: The Case of Ruth Bader
    Ginsburg," *PS: Political Science and Politics* 27, no. 2
    (June 1994).

3. Linda Greenhouse, "Senate, 96-3, Easily Affirms Judge
    Ginsburg as Justice," *New York Times*, August 4, 1993, http://
    www.nytimes.com/1993/08/04/us/senate-96-3-easily-
    affirms-judge-ginsburg-as-a-justice.html.

4. Ibid.

5. John M. Broder, "Edward M. Kennedy, Senate Stalwart, Is
    Dead at 77," *New York Times*, August 26, 2009, http://www.
    nytimes.com/2009/08/27/us/politics/27kennedy.html?_r=0.

Chapter 5

1. "Pay Equity & Discrimination," Institute for Women's Policy
    Research, Accessed November 17, 2016, http://www.iwpr.
    org/initiatives/pay-equity-and-discrimination.

2. "United States v. Virginia 518 U.S. 515 (1996)," Justia, https://
    supreme.justia.com/cases/federal/us/518/515/case.html.

3. "Ruth Bader Ginsburg's Opinions," Columbia Law School,
    https://www.law.columbia.edu/law_school/communications/
    reports/winter2004/opinions.

4. "Supreme Court Upholds ADA 'Integration Mandate' in
    Olmstead Decision," The Center for an Accessible Society,
    June 22, 1999, http://www.accessiblesociety.org/topics/ada/
    olmsteadoverview.htm.

5. "Olmstead v. L.C. 527 U.S. 581 (1999)," Justia, https://supreme.justia.com/cases/federal/us/527/581/case.html.

6. Robert Barnes, "The Forgotten History of Justice Ginsburg's Criticism of *Roe v. Wade*," *Washington Post*, March 2, 2016, https://www.washingtonpost.com/politics/courts_law/the-forgotten-history-of-justice-ginsburgs-criticism-of-roe-v-wade/2016/03/01/9ba0ea2e-dfe8-11e5-9c36-e1902f6b6571_story.html.

7. Ibid.

8. Ibid.

9. Ibid.

10. Danielle Paquette, "Ginsburg Smacks Down a Major Abortion Myth After Historic SCOTUS Ruling," *Washington Post*, June 27, 2016, https://www.washingtonpost.com/news/wonk/wp/2016/06/27/abortion-is-safer-than-childbirth-ruth-bader-ginsburg-writes-after-historic-supreme-court-ruling.

11. Ariana Eunjung Cha, "Supreme Court Rules Against Texas and for Science in Abortion Case," *Washington Post*, June 27, 2016, https://www.washingtonpost.com/news/to-your-health/wp/2016/06/27/the-supreme-court-rules-against-texas-and-for-science-in-abortion-case/?tid=a_inl.

12. Mark Joseph Stern, "RBG Makes Yet Another Brilliant Point About the Constitutional Necessity of Marriage Equality," *Slate*, November 16, 2015, http://www.slate.com/blogs/outward/2015/11/16/ruth_bader_ginsburg_on_gay_marriage_a_constitutional_necessity.html.

13. Alicia Lu, "Ruth Bader Ginsburg's History as a Champion of Gay Rights," *Time*, June 26, 2015, http://time.com/3937882/ruth-bader-ginsburg-gay-marriage-ruling/?xid=tcoshare.

14. Dan Roberts, "Ruth Bader Ginsburg Eviscerates Same-Sex Marriage Opponents in Court," *Guardian*, April 28, 2015, https://www.theguardian.com/us-news/2015/apr/28/ruth-bader-ginsburg-gay-marriage-arguments-supreme-court.

15. Lu, "Ruth Bader Ginsburg's History as a Champion of Gay Rights."

Chapter 6

1. Stefan A. Riesenfeld, "Review of *Civil Procedure in Sweden* by Ruth Bader Ginsburg and Anders Bruzelius," *Columbia Law Review* 67, no. 6 (June 1967).

2. Adam Liptak, "Ginsburg Shares Views on Influence of Foreign Law on Her Court, and Vice Versa," *New York Times*, April 11, 2009, http://www.nytimes.com/2009/04/12/us/12ginsburg.html?_r=0.

3. Ruth Bader Ginsburg, "'A Decent Respect to the Opinions of [Human]kind': The Value of a Comparative Perspective in Constitutional Adjudication," Speech delivered at International Academy of Comparative Law, July 30, 2010, https://www.supremecourt.gov/publicinfo/speeches/viewspeech/sp_08-02-10.

4. Ibid.

5. Ibid.

6. Ryan Park, "What Ruth Bader Ginsburg Taught Me About Being a Stay-at-Home Dad," *Atlantic*, January 8, 2015, http://www.theatlantic.com/business/archive/2015/01/what-ruth-bader-ginsburg-taught-me-about-being-a-stay-at-home-dad/384289.

7. Elias Isquith, "Here Are the Highlights of Justice Ginsburg's Fiery Hobby Lobby Dissent," *Salon*, June 30, 2014, http://www.salon.com/2014/06/30/here_are_the_highlights_of_justice_ginsburgs_fiery_hobby_lobby_dissent/.

8. Eugene Volokh, "Hobby Lobby Wins Before the Supreme Court," *Washington Post*, June 30, 2014, https://www.washingtonpost.com/news/volokh-conspiracy/wp/2014/06/30/scotusblog-reports-closely-held-corporations-cannot-be-required-to-provide-contraception-coverage/?utm_term=.4d487181b715.

9. Greg Stohr, "Ruth Bader Ginsburg Isn't Giving Up Her Fight for Women's Rights," *Bloomberg*, February 12, 2015, http://www.bloomberg.com/news/features/2015-02-12/ruth-bader-ginsburg-isn-t-giving-up-her-fight-for-women-s-rights.

10. "Law Professor Presents Lifetime Achievement Award to Justice Ruth Bader Ginsburg," Oklahoma City University School of Law, January 14, 2013, http://law.okcu.edu/?page_id=30308.

11. Gail Collins, "The Unsinkable R.B.G.," *New York Times*, February 20, 2015, http://www.nytimes.com/2015/02/22/opinion/sunday/gail-collins-ruth-bader-ginsburg-has-no-interest-in-retiring.html.

12. Kendall Breitman, "Ginsburg: I Wasn't '100 Percent Sober' at SOTU," *Politico*, February 13, 2015, http://www.politico.com/story/2015/02/ruth-bader-ginsburg-napping-alcohol-sotu-115172.

13. Joan Biskupic, "Justice Ruth Bader Ginsburg Calls Trump a 'Faker,' He Says She Should Resign," CNN, July 13, 2016, http://www.cnn.com/2016/07/12/politics/justice-ruth-bader-ginsburg-donald-trump-faker.

14. Michael D. Shear, "Ruth Bader Ginsburg Expresses Regret for Criticizing Donald Trump," *New York Times,* July 14, 2016, http://www.nytimes.com/2016/07/15/us/politics/ruth-bader-ginsburg-donald-trump.html.

15. Collins, "The Unsinkable R.B.G."

16. Stohr, "Ruth Bader Ginsburg Isn't Giving Up Her Fight for Women's Rights."

17. Collins, "The Unsinkable R.B.G."

GLOSSARY

ACLU The American Civil Liberties Union is a nonprofit organization that works through the legal and political systems to defend people's individual rights and liberties.

ADA The Americans with Disabilities Act is a civil rights law enacted in 1990 that aims to prevent people with disabilities from being discriminated against.

appellate A court that considers whether to reverse or uphold decisions that have been made in lower court cases. If a decision from a lower court is appealed, it goes to an appellate court.

bar The whole body of attorneys and counselors, or the members of the legal profession, are collectively called "the bar," from the place they usually occupy in court.

brief A written summary of a court case, including the facts and legal points relevant to the case.

deinstitutionalization The systematic removal of people from institutions in an attempt to reintegrate them into the community (in theory, with appropriate supports in place).

egalitarian Supporting the principal that all people are equal and should have equal rights and opportunities.

executive branch The branch of the United States government that ensures laws are followed. The president of the United States is the head of the executive branch.

faute de mieux A French term meaning "for lack of a better alternative."

Founding Fathers The men who led America in the Revolutionary War and ultimately helped form the United States and draft the United States Constitution.

furrier A person who sells furs.

gestation The period of time a fetus is carried in the womb.

haberdasher A person who sells men's clothing.

IRS The Internal Revenue Service is the United States federal tax collection agency.

IUD An acronym for intrauterine device, a type of contraceptive for females that is implanted in the uterus.

jurist An expert in or writer on law

LGBTQ An acronym describing the people who make up the lesbian, gay, bisexual, transgender, and queer community.

McCarthyism The practice of accusing people of treason or subversion regardless of a lack of evidence. During the Cold War, Senator Joseph McCarthy led an effort to persecute many people as Communists without having substantial evidence to back up his theories.

Medicaid waiver Waivers issued by states that allow people with disabilities to receive long-term care services in their home or in a community-based setting, rather than in an institution.

opinion In legal circles, a formal statement that details the reasons why a particular judgment was made.

patriarchal Describing a society controlled by men.

procreation The production of offspring.

self-effacing Modest; not seeking attention for one's successes.

sheltered workshops Supervised workplaces for disabled adults. These workplaces are legally authorized to pay the people who work in them below minimum wage.

widower A man whose spouse has died.

FURTHER INFORMATION

Books

Ginsburg, Ruth Bader, Mary Hartnett, and Wendy W. Williams. *My Own Words*. New York: Simon & Schuster, 2016.

Hirshman, Linda. *Sisters in Law: How Sandra Day O'Connor and Ruth Bader Ginsburg Went to the Supreme Court and Changed the World*. New York: Harper, 2015.

Kanefield, Teri. *Free to Be: Ruth Bader Ginsburg: The Story of Women and Law*. San Francisco: Armon Books, 2016.

Websites

Supreme Court of the United States
https://www.supremecourt.gov

This website provides the text for opinions, oral arguments, decisions, case documents, and much, much more.

Video

Ruth Bader Ginsburg 2016 Master Edit: Academy of Achievement
https://www.youtube.com/watch?v=YCH32n7drMc

BIBLIOGRAPHY

Barnes, Robert. "The Forgotten History of Justice Ginsburg's Criticism of *Roe v. Wade*." *Washington Post*, March. 2, 2016. https://www.washingtonpost.com/politics/courts_law/ the-forgotten-history-of-justice-ginsburgs-criticism- of-roe-v-wade/2016/03/01/9ba0ea2e-dfe8-11e5-9c36- e1902f6b6571_story.html.

———. "How the Other Justices Remember Antonin Scalia." *Washington Post*, February. 14, 2016. https://www. washingtonpost.com/politics/courts_law/how-the-other- justices-remember-antonin-scalia/2016/02/14/30a53ae4- d34b-11e5-9823-02b905009f99_story.html.

Biskupic, Joan. "Justice Ruth Bader Ginsburg Calls Trump a 'Faker,' He Says She Should Resign." CNN, July 13, 2016. http://www.cnn.com/2016/07/12/politics/justice-ruth- bader-ginsburg-donald-trump-faker.

Breitman, Kendall. "Ginsburg: I Wasn't '100 Percent Sober' at SOTU." *Politico*, February 13, 2015. http://www.politico. com/story/2015/02/ruth-bader-ginsburg-napping-alcohol- sotu-115172.

"A Brief Biography of Justice Ginsburg." Columbia Law School. Accessed November 21, 2016. http://www.law.columbia.edu/ law_school/communications/reports/winter2004/bio.

Broder, John M. "Edward M. Kennedy, Senate Stalwart, Is Dead at 77." *New York Times*, August 26, 2009. http://www.nytimes. com/2009/08/27/us/politics/27kennedy.html?_r=0.

Carmon, Irin, and Shana Knizhnik. "'Marty Was Always My Best Friend': Ruth Bader Ginsburg's Love Story." *Jezebel*, October

27, 2015. http://jezebel.com/marty-was-always-my-best-friend-ruth-bader-ginsburgs-l-1738733789.

Cha, Ariana Eunjung. "Supreme Court Rules Against Texas and for Science in Abortion Case." *Washington Post*, June 27, 2016. https://www.washingtonpost.com/news/to-your-health/wp/2016/06/27/the-supreme-court-rules-against-texas-and-for-science-in-abortion-case/?tid=a_inl.

Collins, Gail. "The Unsinkable R.B.G." *New York Times*, February 20, 2015. http://www.nytimes.com/2015/02/22/opinion/sunday/gail-collins-ruth-bader-ginsburg-has-no-interest-in-retiring.html.

Comiskey, Michael. "The Usefulness of Senate Confirmation Hearings for Judicial Nominees: The Case of Ruth Bader Ginsburg." *PS: Political Science and Politics* 27, no. 2 (June 1994): 224–227.

Davidson, Kenneth M., Ruth Bader Ginsburg, and Herma H. Kay. *Sex-Based Discrimination: Text, Case, and Materials*. St. Paul, MN: West Publishing Co., 1974.

Galanes, Philip. "Ruth Bader Ginsburg and Gloria Steinmen on the Unending Fight for Women's Rights." *New York Times*, November 14, 2015. http://www.nytimes.com/2015/11/15/fashion/ruth-bader-ginsburg-and-gloria-steinem-on-the-unending-fight-for-womens-rights.html?_r=1.

Garry, Stephanie. "For Ruth Bader Ginsburg, Hopeful Signs in Grim News About Pancreatic Cancer." *Tampa Bay Times*, February 5, 2009. http://www.tampabay.com/news/health/for-ruth-bader-ginsburg-hopeful-signs-in-grim-news-about-pancreatic-cancer/973728.

Ginsburg, Ruth Bader. "Advocating the Elimination of Gender-Based Discrimination: The 1970s New Look at the Equality Principle." Speech delivered at the University of Cape Town, South Africa, on February 10, 2006. https://www.supremecourt.gov/publicinfo/speeches/sp_02-10-06.html.

———. "'A Decent Respect to the Opinions of [Human]kind': The Value of a Comparative Perspective in Constitutional Adjudication." Speech delivered at International Academy of Comparative Law, American University, on July 30, 2010. https://www.supremecourt.gov/publicinfo/speeches/viewspeech/sp_08-02-10.

———. "Some Reflections on the Feminist Legal Thought of the 1970s." *University of Chicago Legal Forum* no. 1 (1989): 9–21. http://chicagounbound.uchicago.edu/cgi/viewcontent.cgi?article=1047&context=uclf.

———. "US Supreme Court Justice Nomination Acceptance Address." Delivered June 14, 1993. American Rhetoric Online Speech Bank. http://www.americanrhetoric.com/speeches/ruthbaderginsburgusscnominationspeech.htm.

Greenhouse, Linda. "Senate, 96-3, Easily Affirms Judge Ginsburg as a Justice." *New York Times*, August 4, 1993. http://www.nytimes.com/1993/08/04/us/senate-96-3-easily-affirms-judge-ginsburg-as-a-justice.html.

Halberstam, Malvina. "Ruth Bader Ginsburg." Jewish Women's Archive. Accessed November 21, 2016. http://jwa.org/encyclopedia/article/ginsburg-ruth-bader.

Hatch, Orrin. *Square Peg: Confessions of a Citizen-Senator*. New York: Basic Books, 2003.

Isquith, Elias. "Here Are the Highlights of Justice Ginsburg's Fiery Hobby Lobby Dissent." *Salon*, June 30, 2014. http://www.salon.com/2014/06/30/here_are_the_highlights_of_justice_ginsburgs_fiery_hobby_lobby_dissent.

Labaton, Stephen. "The Man Behind the High Court Nominee." *New York Times*, June 17, 1993. http://www.nytimes.com/1993/06/17/us/the-man-behind-the-high-court-nominee.html?pagewanted=all.

Lewis, Neil A. "Ginsburg Promises Judicial Restrain if She Joins Court." *New York Times*, July 21, 1993. http://www.nytimes.

com/1993/07/21/us/the-supreme-court-ginsburg-promises-judicial-restraint-if-she-joins-court.html.

Liptak, Adam. "Ginsburg Shares Views on Influence of Foreign Law on Her Court, and Vice Versa." *New York Times*, April 11, 2009. http://www.nytimes.com/2009/04/12/us/12ginsburg.html?_r=0.

———. "Kagan Says Her Path to Supreme Court Was Made Smoother by Ginsburg's." *New York Times*, February 10, 2014. http://www.nytimes.com/2014/02/11/us/kagan-says-her-path-to-supreme-court-was-made-smoother-by-ginsburg.html?_r=0.

Lu, Alicia. "Ruth Bader Ginsburg's History as a Champion of Gay Rights." *Time*, June 26, 2015. http://time.com/3937882/ruth-bader-ginsburg-gay-marriage-ruling/?xid=tcoshare.

Maloney, Alli. "Five Best Revelations from Gloria Steinem and RBG's Lunch Date." *New York Times*, November 16, 2015. http://nytlive.nytimes.com/womenintheworld/2015/11/16/5-best-revelations-from-gloria-steinem-and-rbgs-lunch-date.

Margolick, David. "Trial by Adversity Shapes Jurist's Outlook." *New York Times*, June 25, 1993. http://www.nytimes.com/1993/06/25/us/trial-by-adversity-shapes-jurist-s-outlook.html?pagewanted=all.

NPR Staff. "Ginsburg and Scalia: 'Best Buddies.'" NPR, February 15, 2016. http://www.npr.org/2016/02/15/466848775/scalia-ginsburg-opera-commemorates-sparring-supreme-court-friendship.

Paquette, Danielle. "Ginsburg Smacks Down a Major Abortion Myth After Historic SCOTUS Ruling." *Washington Post*, June 27, 2016. https://www.washingtonpost.com/news/wonk/wp/2016/06/27/abortion-is-safer-than-childbirth-ruth-bader-ginsburg-writes-after-historic-supreme-court-ruling.

Park, Ryan. "What Ruth Bader Ginsburg Taught Me About Being a Stay-at-Home Dad." *Atlantic*, January 8, 2015. http://www. theatlantic.com/business/archive/2015/01/what-ruth-bader-ginsburg-taught-me-about-being-a-stay-at-home-dad/384289.

"Pay Equity and Discrimination." Institute for Women's Policy Research. Accessed November 21, 2016. http://www.iwpr. org/initiatives/pay-equity-and-discrimination.

Rafei, Roya. "Ruth Bader Ginsburg: The Former Rutgers Law Professor Led the Legal Campaign for Gender Equality." *Rutgers Today*, February 29, 2016. http://news.rutgers. edu/feature/ruth-bader-ginsburg-former-rutgers-law-professor-led-legal-campaign-gender-equality/20160228#.V-Wk7DKZPm0.

Riesenfeld, Stefan A. "Review of *Civil Procedure in Sweden* by Ruth Bader Ginsburg and Anders Bruzelius." *Columbia Law Review* 67, no 6 (June 1967): 1176–1178.

Roberts, Dan. "Ruth Bader Ginsburg Eviscerates Same-Sex Marriage Opponents in Court." *Guardian*, April 28, 2015. https://www.theguardian.com/us-news/2015/apr/28/ruth-bader-ginsburg-gay-marriage-arguments-supreme-court.

Roland, James. *Ruth Bader Ginsburg: Iconic Supreme Court Justice.* Minneapolis: Lerner, 2016.

Rosen, Jeffrey. "The Book of Ruth." *New Republic*, August 1, 1993. https://newrepublic.com/article/61837/the-book-ruth.

"Ruth Bader Ginsburg." Academy of Achievement. Accessed November 21, 2016. http://www.achievement.org/autodoc/page/gin0bio-1.

"Ruth Bader Ginsburg's Opinions." Columbia Law School. Accessed November 21, 2016. https://www.law.columbia. edu/law_school/communications/reports/winter2004/opinions.

Shear, Michael D. "Ruth Bader Ginsburg Expresses Regret for Criticizing Donald Trump." *New York Times*, July 14, 2016. http://www.nytimes.com/2016/07/15/us/politics/ruth-bader-ginsburg-donald-trump.html.

Stern, Mark Joseph. "RBG Makes Yet Another Brilliant Point About the Constitutional Necessity of Marriage Equality." *Slate*, November 16, 2015. http://www.slate.com/blogs/outward/2015/11/16/ruth_bader_ginsburg_on_gay_marriage_a_constitutional_necessity.html.

Stohr, Greg. "Ruth Bader Ginsburg Isn't Giving Up Her Fight for Women's Rights." Bloomberg, February 12, 2015. http://www.bloomberg.com/news/features/2015-02-12/ruth-bader-ginsburg-isn-t-giving-up-her-fight-for-women-s-rights.

"Supreme Court Upholds ADA 'Integration Mandate' in *Olmstead* Decision." The Center for an Accessible Society, June 22, 1999. http://www.accessiblesociety.org/topics/ada/olmsteadoverview.htm.

Swiger, Elinor Porter. *Women Lawyers at Work*. Winter Haven, FL: Messner, 1978.

"Tribute: The Legacy of Ruth Bader Ginsburg and WRP Staff." ACLU. Accessed November 21, 2016. https://www.aclu.org/other/tribute-legacy-ruth-bader-ginsburg-and-wrp-staff.

Volokh, Eugene. "Hobby Lobby Wins Before the Supreme Court." *Washington Post*, June 30, 2014. https://www.washingtonpost.com/news/volokh-conspiracy/wp/2014/06/30/scotusblog-reports-closely-held-corporations-cannot-be-required-to-provide-contraception-coverage/?utm_term=.4d487181b715.

Wood, Margaret. "Women in History: Lawyers and Judges." Library of Congress, March 6, 2015. https://blogs.loc.gov/law/2015/03/women-in-history-lawyers-and-judges.

INDEX

Page numbers in **boldface** are illustrations. Entries in **boldface** are glossary terms.

ABOUT THE AUTHOR

Cathleen Small is an author and editor who lives in the San Francisco Bay Area. She has written two dozen nonfiction books for students on topics such as technology, politics, and war. When she's not writing or editing, Cathleen enjoys traveling with her husband and two young sons.